"Saying the *Pater Noster*

is like swimming in the heart of the sun."

—Thomas Merton, *The Sign of Jonas*

Albert Haase, O.F.M.

Swimming in the Sun:

Discovering the Lord's Prayer
With Francis of Assisi
and Thomas Merton

St.
Anthony
Messenger
Press

Cincinnati, Ohio

Nihil Obstat: Rev. Arthur J. Espelage, O.F.M.
　　　　　　　Rev. Robert L. Hagedorn

Imprimi Potest: Rev. John Bok, O.F.M.
　　　　　　　Provincial

Imprimatur: Rev. R. Daniel Conlon
　　　　　　　Chancellor and Vicar General
　　　　　　　Archdiocese of Cincinnati
　　　　　　　April 30, 1993

The *nihil obstat* and *imprimatur* are a declaration that a book is considered to be free from doctrinal or moral error. It is not implied that those who have granted the *nihil obstat* and *imprimatur* agree with the contents, opinions or statements expressed.

Scripture citations are taken from *The New Revised Standard Version of the Bible*, copyright ©1989 by the Division of Christian Education of the National Council of the Churches of Christ in the USA. Used with permission. All rights reserved.

Cover and book design by Julie Lonneman
Cover illustration by Susan Curtis

ISBN 0-86716-193-0

Published by St. Anthony Messenger Press
Printed in the U.S.A.

(continued on page 216)

Contents

for

Medard Buvala, O.F.M.,

in his fiftieth year of priesthood,
who swims in the sun

Preface

L ike "swimming in the heart of the sun"[1]—that's how
Thomas Merton described his experience of praying
the Lord's Prayer. And that phrase provides a perfect
image for the spirituality I have described in this book.

This spirituality has emerged from my reflections upon
that ancient prayer of Christians, the Lord's Prayer. As such,
it gives attention to three elements not always integrated in
contemporary approaches to spirituality: the importance of
practical experience, psychology and the wisdom of the
world's religions, especially Christianity. It also underscores
what I believe to be the five most important components of
personal spirituality: one's image of God; the present
moment as the place of encounter with God; community;
personal commitment to God's dream of peace, love and
justice; and the practical importance of asceticism. The
major influences upon the book's contents are Francis of
Assisi and Thomas Merton.

Francis of Assisi has been called "everybody's favorite
saint," and his statue continues to be found in birdbaths and
rock gardens everywhere. But beyond the popular image of
the saint stands flesh and blood, consumed with love for God
and charged with Divine grace. This intriguing little

[1] Thomas Merton, *The Sign of Jonas* (New York: Harcourt, Brace and Company,
1953), p. 198.

thirteenth-century Italian felt compelled to live the gospel as literally as he could. By the time he died at age forty-four, he carried in his flesh the crucified wounds of the one he loved so dearly. No wonder Saint Bonaventure called him "another Christ."

Francis's life still challenges us to renounce the superficial and superfluous in our lives, to identify more deeply with the poor and powerless of society, and to have a profound, reverent respect for all creation. Franciscan spirituality is timeless and, as you will discover in these pages, applicable to people of all walks of life.

A portrait of Thomas Merton has been hanging in my bedroom ever since I first read his autobiography, *The Seven Storey Mountain*, in January 1980. On one level our lives as religious crisscrossed: Merton originally applied to the Franciscans, was accepted and then asked to withdraw his application just before entering novitiate. I applied to the Trappists, was accepted and then withdrew my application three months before I was to appear at the monastery gate. But on a deeper level, Merton's life, so graciously and honestly shared with the readers of his autobiography and subsequent journals, has become a vehicle for self-discovery for so many contemporary readers—including me. This twentieth-century monk had the knack for writing from a deep interior place where the lives of many people of different times, religions and interests converge. Thomas Merton, like Francis of Assisi, is one of the great articulators of perennial spiritual wisdom.

I often turn to these two great spiritual masters to illustrate aspects of the spirituality I propose in this book. I could have turned to others and, in fact, in a few places I do. But my familiarity with Francis and Merton, as well as the great trust I have in them to point the way to God, made them the obvious candidates for examples and clarifications.

In addition to Francis of Assisi and Thomas Merton, you will meet other wonderful people in these pages. The names, locations and details of their stories have been changed out of respect for their privacy—with one exception: Father Medard Buvala, O.F.M. This friar, whom I was privileged to live with for three years and whom you will meet in Chapter Five, humbly consented to having all the facts about himself revealed. I have never in all my life known a freer, kinder, more gracious man of God than Med.

Much of this book's material has already been shared with thousands of people in the parish missions and workshops on the spiritual life which I have given across the country. I could never have imagined myself writing this book without their support and encouragement. Thanks also to:

—my family, friends and the friars, especially Daniel Reed, O.F.M., who encouraged me with the oft-repeated question, "How's the book coming along?"

—Kenneth M. Voiles, a budding Merton scholar, who offered helpful comments and suggestions on the original draft.

—Raymond Rickels, O.F.M., who was kind enough to drop everything to help render my complex gobbledygook into English.

—Robert E. Daggy, director of the Thomas Merton Studies Center and affectionately nicknamed "Pontifex Maximus of Things Mertonian," and Anne McCormick, contact person for the Merton Legacy Trust, who helped guide me through the maze of getting permissions to quote from the writings and lectures of Thomas Merton.

—Karen Hurley, the editor of this book, who has the rare ability to change a preacher's words into a reader's delight.

—my sister, Bridget Haase, O.S.U., who offered meticulous suggestions for the book's improvement and, more importantly, whose life inspired the insights of Chapter Seven.

This book is intended to be a popular "handbook" to the spiritual life. It is meant to be read cover to cover, then later reflected upon chapter by chapter. To facilitate the reflections and bring each chapter home to one's personal experience, I have included questions for reflection at the end of each chapter. My hope is that this book will give the reader a glimpse into the unconditional love of God which is that sun in which we really and truly swim.

Albert Haase, O.F.M.

Taishan, Taipei, Taiwan R.O.C.

October 4, 1992
Feast of Saint Francis of Assisi
Forty-fourth anniversary of the publication
of Thomas Merton's *The Seven Storey Mountain*

CHAPTER ONE

Abba! Father!

We will never fathom the mystery of this unique realization. We do not know exactly when it happened to Jesus. As a child? In adolescence? As a young adult? But somewhere along the line, an insight began to blossom: The best way to speak about the intimate love and unconditional acceptance he experienced from Yahweh was to draw upon the familiar language of his own family life. He called Yahweh by the same name he called Joseph, "Abba! Father!"

"Abba" is a Jewish child's name for his father, like "Daddy" or "Pops." It comes out of a deep awareness of one's dependence and need and is spoken out of love. It is also an adult's name for an elderly person who is owed reverence and respect. In both cases, the name suggests immediacy, familiarity, mutual love and self-sacrifice. Unfortunately our English translation "Father" stumbles in carrying the weight of the original "Abba."[2]

Scripture scholars tell us that Jesus was not the first to associate *Abba* with God. An earlier literary tradition describes the action of God "like that of a father." But the Hebrew Scriptures always used the indirect language as if to

[2] I have tried to be sensitive in these pages to the violence of sexist language. I do not, of course, have the freedom to change Merton's sexist language. And my predilection for using Jesus' endearing name for God, "Abba," sometimes corners me into using the masculine pronoun for God.

suggest a promise to be fulfilled someday. No one before Jesus had presumed to take that wooden simile and transform it into a direct address of endearing love. Such religious usage of the direct address was unknown and probably offensive to pious Jews.

By calling God "Abba," Jesus was taking a giant step. One might even call it a risk. Jesus dared to trust his own personal experience of God: a profound experience of Divine love and undivided Divine attention! Like a new parent contemplating a first-born, Yahweh's gaze was riveted upon Jesus and, Jesus insisted, upon each one of us. That experience of God—and Jesus' trust in it—would subsequently shape his entire life.

Jesus' childlike, self-assured intimacy with Yahweh confronted and challenged the spirituality of people like the scribes and Pharisees, sometimes burdened with external obedience to the Law. Jesus turned the spiritual life inside out. The interior quality of the heart superseded fatted calves and burnt offerings. Immanence overshadowed transcendence.

For Jesus, Abba's loving concern and personal investment in each human heart became the primary focus for understanding human behavior: "We love because [God] first loved us" (1 John 4:19).

As Jesus grew in age and wisdom, he centered more and more upon this personal experience of the Divine. Indeed, the loving presence of God as Abba became the central relationship which motivated Jesus and catapulted him into a preaching career. During his preaching ministry he continually withdrew to solitary places to confirm the authenticity of this new revelation of God.

With a presumption that scandalized many pious Jews, Jesus invited his disciples to join him in this shockingly intimate relationship with the Transcendent One. When they asked him for a way to pray, Jesus taught his followers the hallowed prayer that Christians to this day refer to as the "Our Father."

Jesus freely shared with society's outcasts the love and forgiveness of his Abba. Later, with fear and trembling in the Garden of Gethsemane and on the cross, Jesus must have agonized over whether or not he had deceived himself in trusting in this intimate experience of Yahweh as Abba. In the end, however, he trusted again. Surely Abba would not tolerate the annihilation of a loved one.

Our Image of God

Our image of God is one of the most, if not *the* most, important aspects of the spiritual life. Our God-image shapes and colors everything about our personal spirituality: from why we pray to how we understand suffering and evil in the world.

Healthy images of God lead to sanctity. Unhealthy images of God elicit unhealthy behavior. Indeed, a particular image of God can be the very reason someone leaps to holiness or walks at a mere snail's pace in the spiritual life. One definition of holiness is "self-sacrificing openness to the Divine reality." To become holy, then, our image of God must be able to draw out our deepest goodness and help us transcend the boundaries of our ego with its selfish concerns. What kind of God-image can do that?

Scripture says that "the fear of the LORD is the beginning of knowledge" (Proverbs 1:7). Unfortunately, many people understand that in a literal way. They are afraid of God. And their fear is a direct result of their God-image. Many people think of God as the angry lawgiver holding a loaded gun to their heads; as the stern, aloof teacher waiting to rap their knuckles with a ruler; as the picayune cashier who demands payment to the last red penny; as the nit-picking state trooper ticketing each and every violation of the speed limit.

Many people would publicly deny such images of God. They are too childish, too unsophisticated. But the image of a stern and vengeful God is alive and well. You often meet it in the scrupulous person who feels the need to go to confession twice a week "so I won't burn in hell." The stern image is found in the conscience that whispers to the human heart, "I had the accident because God is punishing me for my sins." The vengeful God is proclaimed by the person in the pulpit who says that AIDS is God's punishment upon the gay community. Occasionally, such images are handed down by some parents to their children.

Basil Hume, the Roman Catholic cardinal of England, once told this story about the God-image offered to him in his childhood. His mother wanted to teach him self-discipline. So she called him into the kitchen and said, "Son, I have just finished baking some delicious cookies, and I've put them in this cookie jar. I'm going to leave this cookie jar right here on the table. But don't you dare sneak in here and eat any of them. Remember: God is watching you!"

For years young Basil Hume lived in fear of the ever-watchful "God of the cookie jar." Then one day, long after he had become a monk and was ordained a priest, it suddenly hit him like a ton of bricks: If he had sneaked into that kitchen and put his hand into that cookie jar and secretly eaten one of those cookies, God would have said this: "Basil, they're so good! Have another one!"

Cardinal Hume's story emphasizes a basic fact of the spiritual life sometimes inadvertently overlooked when we talk about God. God is vitally interested and invested in each one of us. So much so, Jesus says, that Abba has counted each individual hair on our heads with eagle-eyed precision (see Matthew 10:30). He says his Abba will respond with "good things" to those who ask (see Matthew 7:7-11). The depth of this caring interest and concern for us can only be described in the language of the deepest human experience: "[God] first loved us" (1 John 4:19). Basil Hume's "God of the chocolate chip cookie" comes closer to Jesus' Abba than the cold, frightening "policeman of the cookie jar" some of us imagine God to be.

The Unconditional Love of God

The Gospels tell us that at his baptism, Jesus had a profound experience of Abba's investment in his life, of unconditional love and being the beloved: "You are my Son, the Beloved; with you I am well pleased" (Mark 1:11).

We too, by baptismal incorporation into the life and death of Christ, share in Jesus' graced relationship to Abba. We are called and chosen as "the beloved," who share in the same unconditional love that Jesus experienced at his baptism. Divine adoption makes each of us a "child of God" having the freedom to address God as "Abba, Father" (Romans 8:15).

"But I'm a sinner! I don't deserve God's love! And how dare I call God a name like 'Daddy'?" Many of us say it in our own way. And it might be true. But we have already captured Abba's attention. We are indeed loved unconditionally as Abba's beloved.

That is probably the hardest fact to absorb in the spiritual life. The unconditional love of Abba is so mind-boggling, in fact, that some people try to rationalize away the "unconditional" part. They say that God loves them "as long as" they are good. They believe that Divine love is conditional and that they have to live up to certain requirements in order to be confident of it. "God cannot love me because I struggle with sexual sin," or "I'll have to change my ways before God could ever take a serious interest in me," or "How can God possibly love someone like me who hasn't been to church in years?"

Writing of the gift of God's unconditional love, Thomas Merton states:

> One of the keys to real religious experience is the shattering realization that no matter how hateful we are to ourselves, we are not hateful to God.... We need to see good in ourselves in order to love ourselves. He does not. He loves us not because we are good, but because He is.[3]

The love of God is not some generous return for our acts of piety and charity. Nor is it payment for services rendered. Rather, God's love is the constitutive reality of human experience. Merton writes:

> For it is God's love that warms me in the sun and God's love that sends the cold rain. It is God's love that feeds me in the bread I eat and God that feeds me also by hunger and fasting. It is the love of God that sends the winter days when I am cold and sick, and the hot summer when I labor and my clothes are full of sweat: but it is God Who breathes on me with light winds off the river and in the breezes out of the wood.[4]

Unlike our fragile human love, the love of God is not fickle and conditional, based upon expectations and hidden agendas. It is literally like the air we breathe. It is inside of us as we exist in it. It is like the rays of the sun which shine

---

[3] Thomas Merton, *The New Man* (New York: Farrar, Straus & Giroux, 1961), p. 96.
[4] Thomas Merton, *New Seeds of Contemplation* (New York: New Directions, 1961), p. 16.

upon us even on the rainiest of days and whose reflection off the moon guides us in the dark of night. We cannot earn it. We cannot live without it. Existence is the abundance of Divine love. As Saint Paul wrote so passionately in his Letter to the Romans:

> I am convinced that neither death, nor life, nor angels, nor rulers, nor things present, nor things to come, nor powers, nor height, nor depth, nor anything else in all creation, will be able to separate us from the love of God in Christ Jesus our Lord. (Romans 8:38-39)

We, like Jesus, are first and foremost the beloved. That awareness should transform us, like Jesus, into lovers.

Experiences of Incarnation

Christmas is *the* feast of an insatiable Divine love for humanity, of a captivated, fixated Lover wanting to be present, wanting to touch and share the very experiences of the beloved, wanting to become what is loved. From the Franciscan perspective, Christmas is not the beginning of righting wrongs or canceling debts. It is the culmination of a love story which began with the dawn of creation.

When twenty-seven-year-old Joseph first sought me out for counseling, he was very depressed. He was running after every cheap thrill he could think of: alcohol, gambling, sex and drugs. He wanted to ease the pain of his own self-hatred. We met only twice. He never showed up for his third appointment.

Then, a year later, I happened to meet Joseph in a shopping mall in Joliet, Illinois. I was surprised. The Joseph I had worried about and so often prayed for seemed no longer to exist. Here was a new Joseph: confident, at peace with himself and with a wonderful sparkle in his eyes. And the more we talked, the more my curiosity got the best of me.

"Joseph, what's happened to you? You seem different." I really wanted to say "changed."

He coaxed me with a bag of popcorn to sit down on a bench in front of the entrance to Sears. And with the reverence of a newly ordained priest proclaiming the Scriptures, Joseph began telling me about Mary Jo.

"I guess she just took a shine to me at first. It really wasn't mutual. And it certainly wasn't love at first sight. But we talked on the phone, did some dating and, somewhere along the line, she blurted out, 'I think I'm in love with you, Joseph.'"

"To be honest, Father, that's when I first really noticed Mary Jo. And a funny thing started happening after she said that. It was like a heavy weight was suddenly taken off my shoulders, like someone freed me from prison. I stopped fighting against life and came out of my depression. Her love not only challenged me to accept myself but, as a result of it, I gradually became the person that I guess I'm meant to be. I went for professional counseling and that opened up the whole new world of feelings and emotions for me. And you know, Father, the next thing I knew, I was in love!"

A few minutes later with tears in his eyes, Joseph added a profound statement which initially passed me by. "When I now think about that first time Mary Jo told me she loved me, I can't help but think that she was looking at me with the eyes of God!"

Jesus does not have the corner on the market of enfleshing Divine love. The Incarnation did not simply happen once and for all, two thousand years ago. Rather, Jesus reveals the dynamic that is continually going on in this life: Abba's unconditional love is constantly taking on flesh and blood.

Joseph's experience of Mary Jo's love, anyone's experience of human love, is not somehow "like" the experience of God's love. It *is* the love of God, though always incomplete and at times broken or even distorted. As Merton once said, "If you love another person, it's God's love being realized. One and the same love is reaching your friend through you, and you through your friend."[5] Whenever a person says to me, "I love you," that person is contemplating me with the eyes of God. Yes, God so loves the world that the saving Word still becomes flesh (see 1 John 3:16).

The Motherhood of God

In the Book of Genesis we read, "God created humankind in his image, in the image of God he created them, male and female he created them" (Genesis 1:27). We twentieth-century Christians have fashioned our image of God with such strong masculine characteristics that we tend to forget the femininity of God—the dimension of the Divine presence that nurtures us, comforts us and holds us in her lap. After all, according to Genesis, the Divine image is male *and* female.

In spite of the patriarchal society in which Jesus was reared, Jesus had an appreciation for the feminine dimension of the Divine. He compared the forgiveness of God to a woman who woke up late at night and swept her house in search of her lost coin (Luke 15:8-10). Speaking of Divine providence, Jesus said God feeds the birds and helps the wildflowers to grow (Matthew 6:26, 28-30), two traditional tasks of women in Jewish, Greek and Roman society. He

[5] David Steindl-Rast, "Man of Prayer," in *Thomas Merton/Monk: A Monastic Tribute*, ed. Brother Patrick Hart (New York: Sheed and Ward, Inc., 1974), p. 88.

compared God's reign over us to the yeast kneaded into dough by women (Matthew 13:33).

Jesus' use of feminine images to describe the motherhood of God could have been inspired by the prophet Isaiah. Isaiah had compared God's relationship with us to that of a mother's relationship with the child of her womb (49:15). Isaiah also stated that God comforts us as a mother comforts her son (66:13).

Like Isaiah—and Jesus—many Christians have continued to use feminine imagery to speak of God. In the second century Clement of Alexandria described God as a mother. In the fourteenth century the English mystic Julian of Norwich wrote at length about God's maternal love and fertile creativity. Thomas Merton also celebrates the femininity of God in her merciful tenderness and love in his poem, "Hagia Sophia":

> All the perfections of created things are also in God; and therefore He is at once Father and Mother. As Father He stands in solitary might surrounded by darkness. As Mother His shining is diffused, embracing all His creatures with merciful tenderness and light. The Diffuse Shining of God is Hagia Sophia. We call her his "glory." In Sophia his power is experienced only as mercy and as love.[6]

Pope John Paul I in his Angelus address of September 10, 1978, said, "God is our Father. Even more, God is our Mother."

Only an image of God which includes both masculine and feminine characteristics can approximate the God to whom Jesus prayed. The Abba of Jesus is strong and tender, loving and compassionate, indulgent and protective—the best of the feminine and the best of the masculine. Abba is

---

[6] Thomas Merton, in *The Collected Poems of Thomas Merton* (New York: New Directions, 1977), p. 367.

Basil Hume's God of the chocolate chip cookie, not the police officer watching over the cookie jar. Abba is the God who incarnates unconditional love in human flesh.

As long as we have an image of God that only instills fear or shame, we have not come to know the Abba of Jesus. The most we can give someone we fear is our respect. But that is a far cry from the wholehearted and spontaneous opening up to the Divine presence that equates with true holiness.

A New Understanding of Prayer

When the Hebrew Scriptures speak of "fear of the Lord," it refers to an awareness of God's loving presence in our lives—it has nothing to do with the negative, vengeful God-image that I spoke of earlier. It is the realization that God is closer to us than we ever suspected or imagined. To borrow from another religious tradition, it is the discovery that "God is closer to me than my own pulse" (the *Koran*). This realization, of course, inspires awe, devotion and reverence. It should lead to the "awe-filled" response of love, not the negative anxiety of dread and trepidation. The Chinese language accurately translates the biblical understanding of "fear of the Lord" with three characters literally meaning "to hold God in awe, to stand in awe of God."

Prayer begins with this "awe-filled" awareness of the loving Divine presence. Simply put, prayer is becoming aware and taking notice of the presence of God in which we dwell and which dwells within us. Prayer is discovering and growing in the conscious awareness of a God who, like a captivated, ever-present parent, continually contemplates, nurtures, indulges and protects. Prayer is "standing in awe of God"; it is expressing "fear of the Lord."

Many of us mistakenly think that God is "out there," and prayer is the process by which we "get" God. We turn God into an object, like a butterfly, that we try to catch in the net of our prayers and spiritual techniques.

We are like the little fish who swam to its mother and said, "Mommy, they were talking about this thing called 'water' today in school. I swam all around looking for it—from the bottom of the ocean to the place where the land meets the sea—but I couldn't find it! Where is this thing called 'water'?"

Many of us want to know, "Where is this thing called 'God'?" But God is not "out there." We are already "in" God. As Catherine of Siena has written, "As the fish is in the ocean and the ocean is in the fish, so are we in God."

God is like the air we breathe. Perhaps that is why the deeper we grow in the prayerful awareness of the Divine presence in our lives, the less we actually say with words and the more we simply breathe and enjoy it. As Merton once told the young monks of Gethsemani:

> The presence of God is like walking out of a door into the fresh air. You don't concentrate on the fresh air. You *breathe* it. And you don't concentrate on the sunlight. You just enjoy it. It's all around you.... The things in life that correspond somewhat to the presence of God are not things on which you *can* concentrate or on which you *do* concentrate. You just simply are *in* them. When you swim, you don't concentrate on the water.... To be in the presence of God is, in a certain sense, like being in water.[7]

It is as if we are the fish swimming in the ocean of Divine love. As Scripture says, "In him we live and move and have our being" (Acts 17:28a). Prayer is growing in the awareness

---

[7] Thomas Merton, "Does God Hear Our Prayer?" (Kansas City, Mo.: Credence Cassettes), tape AA 2071.

of the Divine milieu in which we already exist.

People who "fish" for God often try too hard and end up frustrated. This is a common mistake for the beginner at prayer. While a novice under Merton's guidance, the contemporary spiritual writer and lecturer James Finley was chastised for his over-zealous approach to prayer. Merton's advice was simple yet profound, "Brother, how does an apple ripen? It just sits in the sun."

Such is the life of prayer: sitting in the sun to ripen! Prayer is not a matter of actively doing things to get God. It is the existential awareness of basking and breathing in the Divine presence.

John Vianney told this story of "ripening": An old man visited a village church every day, but he seemed to do nothing. He fingered no rosary, thumbed no prayer book, mumbled no prayers. One day his parish priest asked, "Old man, what do you do when you come to my church every day? I don't see you pray. I don't see you kneel. I don't see you light any candles. What are you doing?"

The old man replied that indeed he was praying.

"How?" asked the priest.

"Well," the old man replied, "I sit here and look at him, and he looks back at me. That's all."

Such is the life of prayer: to bask in the consciousness of Abba's continual gaze. Prayer is not actively searching for God. It is discovering that I have already been found by God. It is becoming aware of the fact that at every moment of my existence Abba is already contemplating me.

Authentic "fear of the Lord" is this conscious awareness of Abba's captivated delight and unconditional love for me. It is the reverent, awe-filled recognition that "God knows I'm here. And that makes a difference to God." It is the realization that I am first and foremost "the beloved." Only then do I become "the lover."

"We love because [God] first loved us" (1 John 4:19).

The Divine Indwelling

Hints of the immediate, intimate awareness of God that Jesus had, though uniquely his own, have also been experienced by some Christians through the centuries. Mystics have written about an interior Divine presence using various images: "the spark of the soul," "the apex of the soul," "the center of the soul," "the interior fire," "the voice within," "the ground of being," "the true self." To rewrite the words of Scripture, "In me, God lives and moves and has Divine being."

Our original parents had an awareness of this Divine indwelling in the Garden of Eden. One of the consequences of Adam and Eve's sin, though, is the loss of that "interior, simple self, our godlike self, the image of God, 'Christ in us.'"[8] We have become distracted, choosing to fix our attention on things thought to be of greater importance. More tragically, we are divided. We are alienated from our very selves. We are no longer centered. Plain and simple, we are lost. As Meister Eckhart, the German Dominican of the fourteenth century, said, "God is at home. It is we who have gone out for a walk."

The journey away from this interior godlike self has created a new center of gravity never intended by the Creator. Thomas Merton called it by various names: "the imaginary self," "the external self," "the self-seeking-self," "the sensual, selfish and exterior self," "the compulsive and automatic self," or "the false self."

[8] Thomas Merton, *Spiritual Direction and Meditation* (Collegeville, Minn.: The Liturgical Press, 1960), p. 28.

The false self, a direct result of original sin, expresses itself in our over-emotional investment in what we do, what we have and what people think of us. It is like a black hole which sucks into itself all of our creative energies. It insists upon controlling, manipulating and dominating. Its concerns are selfish, individualistic and superficial. The false self makes us forget who we really are by causing us to become obsessed with what we are not. Merton believes that all sin starts from the assumption that this false self, with its egocentric agenda, is the fundamental road to happiness in this life.

The parable of the prodigal son (Luke 15:11-32) can be interpreted as a parable about the seduction of the false self and the rediscovery of the true self. The younger son demands an early inheritance, leaves home and makes a new life for himself. Though we might applaud the industrious independence of the son, there is something inherently selfish in the whole affair. But that is the nature of the false self. It feeds upon itself, thrives on instant gratification, is blindly invested in the agenda of the ego and isolates a person from others. This venture ultimately leads the younger son to the pigs, a shocking image of the final destination of those who invest heavily in the false self.

How can the younger son—any one of us—become free from the obsessions and agenda of the false self and thus leave the pig pen where we are truly foreigners? That's where asceticism comes in.

Asceticism

Thomas Merton described asceticism as "the purification and liberation of the divine image in man, hidden under layers of 'unlikeness.'" He continued:

Our true self is the person we are meant to be—the man who is free and upright, in the image and likeness of God. The work of recovery of this lost likeness is effected by stripping away all that is alien and foreign to our true selves—shedding the "double garment" of hypocrisy and illusion by which we try to conceal the truth of our misery from ourselves, our brethren and from God.[9]

Eleven years later Merton used a Pauline image to convey the same understanding:

In any case, the "death of the old man" is not the destruction of personality but the dissipation of an illusion, and the discovery of the new man is the realization of what was there all along, at least as a radical possibility, by reason of the fact that man is the image of God.[10]

Asceticism is the conscious shedding of the illusions which the false self adamantly claims to be realities. It is dropping the crutches and personality props that the ego insists are necessary life-support systems. It is breaking free from the magnetic hold of the ego by following Jesus' exhortation to "die to the [false] self." Using the imagery of the prodigal son parable, asceticism is abandoning life with the pigs and returning home to the center, to the godlike self, where Abba waits with ring, robe and fatted calf.

A Zen master once described the purpose of Zen as "dismounting and getting off the ass—*and you're the ass!*" Most of us do go through life riding the stallion of the ego and yelling, "Here I come! Make way for me! Coming through!" We need to "get off our high horse" and return home.

Asceticism liberates my divine image, the "Christ in me."

[9] Thomas Merton, *The Silent Life* (New York: Farrar, Straus, and Cudahy, 1957), p. 22.
[10] Thomas Merton, *Zen and the Birds of Appetite* (New York: New Directions, 1968), p. 118.

It shows me the way home to my true self. It is the labor pains of being "born again." It is discovering "my original face before I was born," as the Zen masters say. It is responding to the call of Jesus: "[T]hose who lose their life for my sake will find it" (Matthew 16:25). It is becoming aware of a treasure hidden in a field and selling all to possess it (Matthew 13:44).

The Great Insight

Asceticism makes us receptive to the great insight of the spiritual life: There is nothing "to get" because we already have it! As Merton says:

> In prayer we discover what we already have. You start where you are and you deepen what you already have, and you realize that you are already there. We already have everything, but we don't know it and we don't experience it. Everything has been given to us in Christ. All we need is to experience what we already possess.[11]

The great treasure exposed by prayer is our godlike self, the image of God, Christ in us. It is a pure gift from God. A few years before he died, Merton tried to describe the treasure:

> At the center of our being is a point of nothingness which is untouched by sin and by illusion, a point of pure truth, a point or spark which belongs entirely to God, which is never at our disposal, from which God disposes of our lives, which is inaccessible to the fantasies of our own mind or the brutalities of our own will. This little point of nothingness and of *absolute poverty* is the pure glory of God in us. It is so to speak His name written in us.... It is like a pure diamond,

---

[11] Steindl-Rast, p. 80.

blazing with the invisible light of heaven. It is in everybody....[12]

Once while speaking on this topic during a week-long workshop on prayer and the spiritual life, I was publicly challenged by an articulate, well-read woman. She accused me of preaching some form of New Age spirituality under the appearance of Christian mysticism. "I am not God—nor even a god! This is heresy!"

This woman voiced an uneasiness that many feel when they are confronted with the experiences of Christian mystics. But ponder Merton's description carefully: He says this pristine, interior point "belongs entirely to God." No human being can claim it as his or her own. It is "inaccessible" because it is not a "thing." One does not reach it through mental gymnastics or sheer, brutal force of desire. It is clearly a gift, a grace, that comes with the reality of birth. As the woman so correctly said, "I am not God—nor even a god." Yet God does dwell within me, within you.

The seventeenth-century Spanish mystic, John of the Cross, writes in his *Ascent to Mount Carmel* that this interior Divine indwelling is the very source of a person's existence:

> God sustains every soul and dwells in it substantially, even though it may be that of the greatest sinner in the world. This union between God and creatures always exists. By it God conserves their being so that if the union would end, they would immediately be annihilated and cease existing.[13]

But lest anyone misread the great Carmelite saint, he goes on to add that the soul continues to remain distinct from God, "just as a window, although illumined by a ray of light,

---

[12] Thomas Merton, *Conjectures of a Guilty Bystander* (Garden City, N.Y.: Doubleday and Company, 1966),p. 142.
[13] *Ascent to Mount Carmel*, Book 2, 5:3.

has an existence distinct from the ray."[14] Asceticism is the process of cleaning the window and letting the sun shine through.

Conversion

Authentic conversion begins when a person experiences the initial glimmer of the great insight. *The New Revised Standard Version* translates the conversion moment in the life of the prodigal son in these poignant terms: "he came to himself" (Luke 15:17). To come back to the true self is to come back home to the interior sanctuary where the Divine presence dwells; it is to recover the original stance of Adam and Eve. This experience is an earthquake which shakes the very foundation of the false self and often produces irreparable cracks in it. We suddenly become aware and rediscover who we really are and what we already have.

Merton confesses that his own conversion began "with the realization of the presence of God *in this present life*, in the world and in myself, and that my task as Christian is to live in full and vital awareness of this ground of my being and of the world's being."[15] Conversion and asceticism end one's self-imposed exile and lead a person back to the center, to the ground of being, where one is open to the presence of Jesus' Abba.

Suffering

Emotional suffering can play an important role in the journey home when harnessed as a transforming power. Ninety-five per cent of recovering alcoholics say that it was

[14] Ibid., 5:7.
[15] Merton, *Conjectures of a Guilty Bystander*, pp. 292-293.

emotional pain which motivated them to admit their powerlessness over alcohol and seek help. People end destructive, codependent relationships when the emotional anguish becomes unbearable. Seeking out needed psychological help is motivated by deep-seated emotional pain. Emotional suffering is often the stimulus for change.

Ironically, so much emotional pain, frustration and anxiety are self-imposed. They are direct results of making the conscious decision to remain with the pigs, to continue riding our high horses, to preserve and protect the agenda of the false self. Emotional stress and anxiety come from the ego's adamant compulsion to dominate and control life and other people. Emotional suffering can be the price we pay to keep the false self alive. Until we realize that, we point fingers of accusation and mistakenly blame others for our frustrations and hurts.

One of the most important effects of physical and emotional suffering is the way it challenges and reshapes personal God-images. Indeed, our personal image of God is often carved out of our wounds. Chemical addiction, physical disability, emotional turmoil, terminal illness or mid-life restlessness—all these can often provide an opportunity for the manifestation of the personal God of adult life. Suffering can be a Divine epiphany.

By the time I met Allen, AIDS had already stripped him of his rugged good looks and healthy body weight. He was bedridden, frail and eager to tell me about his journey to God.

"I've known something wasn't right with me since I was in third or fourth grade. In high school I realized that my problem was being gay—and I was deeply ashamed of that. Try as I did, I just couldn't accept it. And at the same time, I just couldn't fake being straight. The more I begged and pleaded with God to change me, the more I felt ashamed and dirty and messed up. So I guess it was a way of dealing with my shame that I just gave up on God. I decided to run away from him. That way I wouldn't be reminded of the eternal punishment that I was told I would get for being gay.

"However, things began to change when I got sick. Everything was gradually pulled from underneath my feet. My family and friends became strangely scarce. My dignity disappeared. Then my financial security. And finally my independence.

"I still remember the day when I hit rock bottom. I was thoroughly depressed and lonely. To my own surprise, I turned to God. 'This is Allen, God. Remember me?' I said. Though I suspected God was aware of my struggles and frustration with sexuality, I also wanted to make sure God knew the hurt he had caused me. I was angry and I wanted God to know it. After all, by this time I had nothing to lose.

"The Church has continually told me that I am expected to live as a celibate or married to a woman. Even a fool knows how impossible and absurd either choice would have been for me. So I told God just how cruel it was, to make me in such a way that I would never get into heaven. I yelled at God for stacking the cards against me from the moment of my birth.

"And you know what? Instead of discovering an unfeeling judge, I found a loving Father who understood, who cared, who was more concerned about *me* than about how I had lived! And he had been with me all the time—in every one-night stand and every doctor's appointment. I might have been running, but he stayed put. He was here all along waiting for me.

"AIDS has forced me to let go of so many things that I thought were so important. But surprisingly, the more I let go and surrender, the more I find God to be a loving Father who is closer to me than I could have ever imagined."

Adult Images of God

We do not let go of our childhood images of God easily. They are rooted deep in our bones. And when those early images are oddly distorted or downright perverted, one's spiritual life in adulthood, if it exists at all, can be adversely affected.

Many people find themselves at the same crossroads as Cardinal Hume and Allen: Many have to choose between an image of God handed down to them by someone else and an image of God revealed in their own personal experiences of human life. The easier choice, often, is to believe in the God-image that one has been given in the home or classroom. I have therefore come to respect deeply people like Allen who take the great leap of faith—sometimes with fear and trembling—and place their trust in the deeply personal revelations of God in their lives. Such personal religious experiences have a way of correcting the errors of our upbringing and education.

As a child, I worshiped the ground my father walked on. Of his three sons and two daughters, I was unquestionably his favorite. But when I was thirteen years old, my father committed suicide. That gunshot wound not only killed my father. It also shattered the image of God that I had been given early in my life. The all-powerful, ever-present God of the *Baltimore Catechism* not only appeared powerless before my tragedy but also seemed coldly disinterested and far away.

One day in my mid-twenties, after years of searching for a father's love, I cried out in prayer to the God of my childhood, to the all-powerful, ever-present God of the *Baltimore Catechism.* I demanded an explanation, reasons, an answer to the "Why?" that continued to gnaw away at my soul. And the response to my prayer? Cold silence. Detached indifference. My childhood God seemed dead.

But then something happened. Out of the blue I felt myself surrounded by a loving comfort and a protective care that I previously had never experienced. It felt as if someone was cradling me in tender arms and holding me tight. Though the pain and memory of my father's death were still very much present, I knew I wasn't alone in my suffering. And indeed, I wasn't. On a Thursday afternoon in 1981, my personal God—the God of Albert Haase—revealed himself to me.

That experience has radically changed my personal image of God. I no longer think of God as a cold, aloof Creator who has abandoned me here on earth. I no longer believe God to be an insensitive judge who rules all creation heartlessly. My new God-image has been carved out of my wound and based upon an experience of God's love for me. God is now the Abba of Jesus—a God of boundless love, consolation and compassion who continually surrounds me. Like a Divine mother, God nurtures and nourishes me in times of pain and loneliness. Like a Divine father, God offers me strength and courage when I need them. And God is so close to me that my other needs are often anticipated even before I myself am aware of them.

This new image of God has been with me for over a decade. But I know it, too, will change. The Divine presence, as blatantly as a sunrise in spring or as subtly as a pat on the back on a lonely day, continually reveals itself. Consequently, these religious experiences will challenge me again to refine my personal image of God.

We outgrow our images of God like we do our clothes and shoes. If we do not continually refine and update them as a result of our personal experiences of God, we run the risk of dreadful God-images ("Suicide must be the will of God"), a childish spirituality, or even worse, the radical disbelief of atheism or agnosticism. The closer we get back home through asceticism, the better sight we have of the God waiting for us.

The Conversion of Francis of Assisi

Brother Thomas of Celano, the first biographer of Francis of Assisi, describes Saint Francis' conversion in his *First Life*. In the first fifteen paragraphs Celano paints a portrait of Francis as "an example to all of conversion to God." A close look at these paragraphs provide concrete expression of the themes explored in this chapter.

For twenty-five years the young Francis squandered both time and money. He outdid his friends in vanity, vainglory, popularity and fine clothes. Francis focused his creative energies upon making a name for himself. His proud, extravagant father must have been pleased to see that "the apple did not fall far from the tree." Francis' false self was alive and well. Indeed, it was thriving.

But then Francis experienced the cross. A period of mental distress and bodily suffering began to awaken his senses to another reality. Initially, he could not comprehend this new reality: He only knew he was a stranger and an exile in a foreign land. Celano tells us that Francis "began to despise himself and to hold in some contempt the things he had admired and loved before."

The false self, however, is unyielding. Its compulsion is to make itself perceptible to the world and to construct its agenda as the sanctuary of meaning for one's life. So Francis still kept alive the hope of accomplishing great deeds of worldly glory and vanity. He vowed to go to Apulia with a nobleman from Assisi in hopes of attaining glory as a knight. Though a vision seemed to confirm future success, the restless Francis felt ambivalent. His heart was resisting. "He was not filled with his usual happiness over such things," Celano comments.

Francis gradually recognized the lie of military glory. He abandoned the idea of going to war and, instead, started the interior spiritual journey. He became aware and took notice of the Divine presence within. Celano says Francis "withdrew for a while from the bustle and the business of the world and tried to recognize Jesus Christ dwelling within himself." He was soon "afire within himself with a divine fire." He also became aware of God's captivated delight in him and realized that his past "had offended the eyes of God's majesty." Francis had taken the first step towards home, towards the true self, towards God.

Francis quickly lost his appetite for the delights of the false self. Celano tells us, for example, that he "cared no more for money than for the dust." But the obsession with the values of the false self was not broken definitively until Francis stood before the Bishop of Assisi and renounced the possessions given him by his father. When Celano revised his version of this event eighteen years later in the *Second Life*, he placed this short, telling speech in the mouth of the saint:

> From now on I can freely say "Our Father who art in heaven," not "father Pietro Bernardone," to whom, behold, I give up not only the money, but all my clothes too. I will

therefore go naked to the Lord.[16]

To address God as Abba in prayer is to proclaim God as
Abba by the way one lives. That became the mission of
Francis of Assisi. No wonder Brother Conrad of Offida
remembers Francis telling Brother Leo, "I do not consider
the person who is reluctant to say 'Our Father' to be a friar
minor."[17]

We do not know what image of God Francis possessed
before his conversion. If he had one at all, it probably did not
elicit any great emotional response from him. What did elicit
a response, though, was his father's lesson that happiness
was found in experiencing and hoarding the pleasures and
treasures of the world. The young Francis had believed that.
But at 25 Francis' own experience began to betray the lie of
his father's values. So Francis began to renounce them. In
doing so, he began to open himself to the Divine presence
and to image God as one who demanded exactly the opposite
of his father's selfish value system. The God of the adult
Francis was the Divine Almsgiver. Like so many of us,
Francis carved his image of God from the wounds of his
youth.

Sunday after Sunday we go to church. And there we find
as many different images of God as there are people in the
pew. Whether we are consciously aware of it or not, each of
us has painted an image of God upon our hearts. That image,
always a result of the gift of religious experience, has
sometimes been framed by the blood, sweat and tears of our
past. And yet, as different as our personal God-images are,

[16] Thomas of Celano, *Second Life of St. Francis* 12, *St. Francis of Assisi: Writings
and Early Biographies, English Omnibus of the Sources for the Life of St. Francis*
(Franciscan Press, Quincy College, Quincy, Ill.: 1991),p. 372.
[17] *Verba Fr. Conradi*, ed. by Paul Sabatier, *Opuscules de critique historique*, tome
I (Paris: Librarie Fischbacher, 1903),p. 378.

nevertheless, we stand united as the beloved, "daring to pray" in the words of Jesus: "Our Father...."

Points for Reflection

What is my present image of God? How has it grown out of my religious experience? What role has tragedy and disappointment played in shaping it?

Do I "fear" God with reverence or "fear" God with dread? Is God the "policeman of the cookie jar" or the "God of the chocolate chip cookie"?

When have I experienced the masculinity of God? The femininity of God?

What have I learned from my experiences of incarnation?

When have I experienced Abba's captivated contemplation of my being? When have I experienced the Divine presence within?

How do I practice the challenge of asceticism in my life? Are my ascetical practices "leading me home" to the presence of Abba in my life, or are they feeding the pride of the false self?

CHAPTER TWO

'Our Father'

The old teacher of wisdom called over his two disciples and said, "My sons, how can you tell that the night is truly over and the day is dawning?"

The new disciple, anxious to flaunt his spiritual depth after a month of training, instantly replied, "When you see a tree in the distance and can tell whether it is an apple tree or a pear tree. Then you know the day is dawning."

The elderly teacher shook his head. "No."

The other young disciple, more cautious yet just as eager to justify the past year of instruction before his companion, thought for a moment and replied, "When you see an animal in the distance and can tell whether it is a dog or a sheep. Then you know the night is over."

The old teacher, betraying his disappointment with a raised eyebrow, shook his head. "No."

So the two disciples protested. "Tell us, venerable teacher, when is the night over and the day dawning?"

With all the wisdom of the ages, the old teacher spoke deliberately. "My sons, the night is truly over and the day is really dawning when you can look into the eyes of another human being and recognize there your brother or your sister. Until then, it is still night, no matter what time it is."

The first word of the Lord's Prayer carries the weight of creation and yet, we rarely reflect upon it. It stands in direct opposition to the sins of discrimination, apartheid and environmental abuse. It reveals one of the great illuminations in the spiritual life: the experience of the family of humanity, the family of creation.

Prejudice and discrimination are overt expressions of the false self since they classify people as objects and judge them on nothing deeper than superficial appearances. They isolate me from the rest of humanity and arrogantly promote my cause for canonization. They convince me that you and I are fundamentally different. As a result, a wide abyss begins to open up between my side of the tracks and your side of the tracks. This wide abyss becomes the breeding grounds for suspicions and irrational fears. Walls go up. Signs are posted: "No Trespassing." "Keep Out." "Men Only." I look at you as an inferior object. I talk about you and treat you like a thing.

Thomas Merton's poem, "Macarius and the Pony," reveals the power of prejudice to turn people into objects. It is based on a story about Macarius, a fourth-century desert father who cured a young girl who had been changed into a mare.

> People in a village
> At the desert's edge
> Had a daughter
> Who was changed (they thought)
> By magic arts
> Into a pony.
>
> At first they berated her
> "Why do you have to be a horse?"
> She could think of no reply.
> So they led her out with a halter
> Into the hot waste land
> Where there was a saint
> Called Macarius
> Living in a cell.

"Father" they said
"This young mare here
Is, or was, our daughter.
Enemies, wicked men,
Magicians, have made her
The animal you see.
Now by your prayers to God
Change her back
Into the girl she used to be."

"My prayers" said Macarius,
"Will change nothing,
For I see no mare.
Why do you call this good child
An animal?"

But he led her into his cell
With her parents:
There he spoke to God
Anointing the girl with oil;
And when they saw with what love
He placed his hand upon her head
They realized, at once.
She was no animal.
She had never changed.
She had been a girl from the beginning.

"Your own eyes
(Said Macarius)
Are your enemies.
Your own crooked thoughts
(Said the anchorite)
Change people around you
Into birds and animals.
Your own ill-will
(said the clear-eyed one)
Peoples the world with specters."[18]

---

[18] Thomas Merton, "Macarius and the Pony," in *The Collected Poems of Thomas Merton*, pp. 317-318.

Prejudice distorts my vision of other people, transforming them into beasts which must be tamed or fixed. It blinds me to their humanity and to the familial relationship I share with them. After all, Abba is "our" Father.

God as Trinity

One of the first mysteries of the faith which we were taught as children is that God is Trinity: Father, Son and Holy Spirit. Though we were taught it is impossible to explain the meaning of the Trinitarian mystery, Trinity at least alerted us to the "relational essence" of Divinity. The Father loves the Son; the Son loves the Father; and their very relationship is bonded together by the Holy Spirit. The very essence of our God is loving relationships. "God is love" (1 John 4:8).

That doctrine also speaks volumes about the nature of the true self. For if I am created in the image and likeness of this Trinitarian God, then I must also be in loving relationships to be my authentic self. The image and likeness of God stamped upon humanity points to our existential need to be in relationship. We were created to be inextricably bound together. The true self, the godlike self, is relational.

Adam and Eve were created for one another. This was the great insight symbolized by the writer of the second creation account. We must be in relationship to discover who we really are. "Therefore a man leaves his father and his mother and clings to his wife, and the two of them become one flesh" (Genesis 2:24).

Merton saw that the same analogy of complementarity could provide the rationale for a Christian approach to race relations. He believed that different races and cultures *"mutually complete one another."*[19] Writing about the racial tensions of America during the 1960's, Merton wrote:

> White calls for black just as black calls for white. Our significance as white men is to be seen *entirely* in the fact that all men are not white. Until this fact is grasped, we will never realize our true place in the world, and we will never achieve what we are meant to achieve in it. The white man is *for* the black man: that is why he is white. The black man is for the white man: this is why he is black.[20]

We catch glimpses of our true self only in loving relationship to God and others. That is the meaning of Eve sharing one of Adam's ribs (Genesis 2:21-34). That is what the parents of the girl were able to glimpse thanks to a relationship with Macarius. And that's what different races discover in dialogue with one another.

That is why Jesus combined two Mosaic laws into the "greatest commandment": love of God (Deuteronomy 6:5) and love of neighbor (Leviticus 19:18, Mark 12:29-31). We stand authentically as individual human beings only when we stand with our entire family, side by side with Brother Jesus and our other brothers and sisters all over the earth, before the one God who is "our" Abba.

Classic Franciscan spirituality makes the same point. The story is told of how Francis and his followers encountered Lady Poverty whom they invited to their evening meal in typical Franciscan fashion. After a very simple meal of bran bread and water, Lady Poverty asked for a tour of their cloister. The friars took their special guest up a hill and, pointing to the whole world as far as they could see, said,

---

[19] Thomas Merton, *Seeds of Destruction* (New York: Farrar, Straus & Giroux, Inc., 1964), p. 61.
[20] Ibid.

"This, Lady, is our cloister."[21]

When Thomas Merton first entered the walled cloister of the Trappists, he was a severe young monk who had truly renounced the world. His choice for God and the monastery meant a renunciation of humanity and Madison Avenue. In the early years he gave this advice to readers of *Seeds of Contemplation*:

> Do everything you can to avoid the amusements and the noise and the business of men.... Do not read their newspapers unless you are really obliged to keep track of what is going on. Newspapers are a penance, not a diversion. Be glad if you can keep beyond the reach of their radios.... Do not complicate your life by looking at the pictures in their magazines.[22]

Later Merton would comment that this early period in his religious life was marked by a rigid, arbitrary, dualistic separation between God and the world. But this was nothing new for the Catholic piety of the 1940's.

As Merton grew in the spiritual life, however, he realized that even the monk was called to a relationship *with* the world. The true self is always relational. When he published the revised *New Seeds of Contemplation*, he deleted the references to newspapers and magazines in the above-mentioned text. The mature monk realized that he—and all of us—are obliged to keep track of what is going on.

Living as a hermit for the last two years of his life, Merton kept the windows of his hermitage open to the whole world. He wrote about the scandal of nuclear arms, the Vietnam War and the volatile race relations between African-Americans and whites in the South. His vocation as a

[21] The story can be found in the *Sacrum Commercium, Omnibus of the Sources for the Life of St. Francis*, p. 1593.

[22] Thomas Merton, *Seeds of Contemplation* (Norfolk, Conn.: New Directions Books, 1949), p. 46.

Christian demanded that he be in the world and relating to it. He prayed with one eye on Scripture and the other on the daily newspaper. Like Francis, Merton came to see the whole world as his cloister. To quote the title of one of his poems, Merton lived his life "With the World in My Blood Stream."

The Prayer of Intercession

I, too, stand before Abba "with the world in my blood stream." My true self is in union with the family of humanity with its worries and concerns—and, true to that self, I pray the prayer of intercession.

Many people mistakenly believe that the purpose of intercessory prayer is to change the mind of God or make God aware of a particular problem that needs special attention. But as Merton remarked, "We are not rainmakers, but Christians."[23]

Intercessory prayer is an expression of my relationship to the world. I stand before "our" Father and proclaim my connectedness, unity and attachment to the world. "It's simply a need for me to express my love by praying for my friends; it's like embracing them," said Merton.[24]

Intercessory prayer is one way of bridging the gap between all that separates me from my brothers and sisters: economics, education, power, race, religion and culture. To intercede for others before Abba is an expression of my belief in the family of humanity. It is also a landmark on the road toward home.

The absence of the prayer of intercession in one's spiritual life is a poignant indicator of the false self. Only the false self can pray with eyes closed to the sufferings of the

[23] Steindl-Rast, p. 88.
[24] Ibid.

world, with ears deaf to the cries of the hungry and with a heart callous and insensitive to the needs of the human family. Only the false self prays to "my" Father. It's always midnight in the soul of one who fails to pray for the hopes and dreams of the world.

'Splanchnizein'

The importance of compassionate intercession was one of the points that Jesus was trying to make in his parable about the good Samaritan (Luke 10:29-37). A man is robbed and left to die in a ditch. Two law-observant Jews, a priest and a Levite, both deliberately pass him by. But then a foreigner, a Samaritan, comes along. Considered an outcast by Judaism, this Samaritan no doubt knows the feeling of "being left behind to die." He offers a hand of mercy and compassion that goes beyond mere charity and philanthropy. We can almost hear him say to the man in the ditch, "I know what it's like. I've been there."

The Greek verb that Jesus uses for the good Samaritan's mercy and compassion is *splanchnizein*. It is the same word the Evangelists use to describe Jesus' pity and compassion (see Matthew 9:36, 15:32, 20:34; Mark 1:41, 6:34, 8:2; Luke 10:33).

The Greek *splanchnizein* is derived from the noun for "entrails," "bowels," "guts," as the seat of emotions. Compassionate intercession, therefore, comes "from the depths" of a person. The Greek word also connotes a feminine quality since it is occasionally associated with the Hebrew word for "womb," *rechem*. Compassionate intercession therefore emerges from the place where life begins. I immediately think of birthing mothers and how they witness to the inextricable bond of pain and new life.

Authentic compassion and intercession are not superficial forays of the busy-body into the problems of other people. They are not experiences which bloat the ego with good feelings about itself. Rather, compassion and intercession are the natural and spontaneous responses of the true self as it stands in relationship to the world. The true self feels "in its depths" the pains and sorrows of others as they struggle to live a fuller dimension of life. It responds with the power of charity and love. This response, painful as it can be, helps to push the less fortunate out of their darkness and into the light. The true self is constantly in labor. "[W]e ourselves, who have the first fruits of the Spirit, groan inwardly..." (Romans 8:23).

Transforming Stone Into Flesh

The false self remains at a distance from the sufferings of others. It is content to be a spectator. Or it just walks away. It is cold, insensitive, callous. It rationalizes: "Why should I go and share in the pain and sufferings of others? After all, I don't need any more sorrow in my life."

The true self, on the other hand, is involved in the cares and concerns of the world. It is relational. It knows that lack of involvement can be a silent participation in evil. It knows that the labor pains of compassion and intercession are life-giving.

Because of my own experience of being left behind by suicide, I have experienced compassion's life-giving power as I listen to others struggling to pick up the pieces after the suicide of a loved one. There was Delores left behind by an older brother whom she loved dearly and who committed suicide. There was Shirley and the tangled guilt she felt over the suicide of her son, Michael. I remember Peter struggling to survive after the suicide of his wife, Alice. In each and every instance I simply sat, listened and lived through the pain of my own father's suicide all over again. I could truly say, "I know what it's like. I've been there." And my com-passion ("suffering with") brought forth a fuller experience of life for Delores, Shirley and Peter.

Every day the labor pains of compassion and intercession are pushing others into life and light: A recovering alcoholic helps someone else in the sponsor system of Alcoholics Anonymous. A widow pauses to write a tender note of sympathy to a woman who has just lost her husband. Someone who has suffered the trauma of divorce reaches out to others going through that or a similar transition. Through support groups like Adult Children of Alcoholics, people help one another sort through the emotional damage done by the past. In each and every case, one person's pain and suffering become life-giving, "redemptive," for someone else.

Remember your suffering. It need not be in vain. It can become the womb of compassion.

The true self's compassion makes us aware of who we truly are as it bonds us to others in relationships. It helps us to grasp an intuition into the unity shared between a mother and the child in her womb. It provides a real experience of the family of humanity. It makes a heart more loving, more tender and, in the end, more human. Compassion changes a heart of stone into a heart of flesh. It is an existential witness to the world that God is "our" Abba.

The Heart of Holiness

Jesus' actions shook the very foundation of traditional Jewish piety, the observance of the Law. He often appeared to act like a sinner, not a savior. The Gospels note instances when Jesus shattered the legalistic interpretation of the third commandment (Mark 2:23-3:6) or the cultural and social restrictions forbidding public conversations with foreigners and women (John 4:4-30).

Such transgressions against a legalistic mentality were apparently deliberate. When questioned about his disciples' lack of attention to the ritual purity laws of Judaism, Jesus explained his perspective:

> Listen to me, all of you, and understand: there is nothing outside a person that by going in can defile, but the things that come are what defile.... For it is from within, from the human heart, that evil intentions come: fornication, theft, murder, adultery, avarice, wickedness, deceit, licentiousness, envy, slander, pride, folly. All these evil things come from within, and they defile a person. (Mark 7:14-15, 21-23)

The sins Jesus mentions are primarily social in nature. They originate from the lack of loving relationships or caring involvement in the lives of others. They point to a heart that is selfish, callous, insensitive, possessive and defensive. They point directly to the black hole of the false self.

According to Jesus, holiness is based upon the size of one's heart, upon love of God and love of neighbor. The more a person's heart is open and attached to the needs and desires of the poor, the hungry, the disadvantaged and the oppressed, the more that person reflects the true self. And the more one expresses the open heart's attachment in any form of compassionate intercession, the more that person grows in the image of God.

Jesus challenges us to move beyond a "contract approach" to holiness. Legalistic concerns about obeying laws and commandments are not enough. To those Galatians, tempted to place their religious justification on the fulfillment of the law of circumcision, Paul wrote:

> You who want to be justified by the law have cut yourselves
> off from Christ; you have fallen away from grace. For
> through the Spirit, by faith, we eagerly wait for the hope of
> righteousness. For in Christ Jesus neither circumcision nor
> uncircumcision counts for anything; the only thing that
> counts is faith working through love.... For you were called
> to freedom, brothers and sisters; only do not use your
> freedom as an opportunity for self-indulgence, but through
> love become slaves to one another. For the whole law is
> summed up in a single commandment, "You shall love your
> neighbor as yourself." (5:4-6, 13-14)

The spiritual center of the Christian is within, not without. It is the heart, not the commandments. Put another way, we followers of Christ are challenged to stretch the size of our hearts to match that of the God in whose image and likeness we were made. And the tender, loving, compassionate heart of Abba is as big as the whole world.

The Chinese character *shiang*, meaning "to think" or "to ponder," offers an interesting insight for those who reflect upon the past day's events during an examination of conscience or who are preparing for the Sacrament of Reconciliation. The character consists of the ideogram "to inspect" placed above the ideogram for "the heart." The picture speaks a thousand words, doesn't it? Perhaps we spend too much time looking at our observance of the law and fail to inspect the quality of our hearts.

In the Christian life charity takes precedence and is the goal of any external conformity to laws. "Love is the fulfilling of the law" (Romans 13:10). It incorporates all the teachings of Jesus and keeps everything in perspective. Charity is the one virtue upon which we will be judged (see Matthew 25:31-46). In the words of Franciscan Margaret of Cortona, "The way of salvation is easy. It is enough to love."

Hospitality

Hospitality is a concrete way we stretch the size of our hearts. It is an important witness to our conviction that God is "our" Father and we are all one family. Through hospitality—in word, action, silence—I can convey to others the simple fact that there is room in my life for them.

Such hospitality was one of the unique characteristics of the earliest expression of the Franciscan ideal. Francis accepted anyone and everyone who came to the fraternity. All were welcomed. There was room for everybody: rich and poor; noble and peasant; cleric, uneducated and lay.

Chapter seven of the Rule of 1221 challenged Francis' followers to extend that same hospitality to every person whom they encountered. "Whoever comes to them, friend or foe, thief or robber, should be received with kindness."

Hospitality also has another dimension. After we make room for others, we must then give them permission to be who they are without lying. Hospitality is the human expression of God's unconditional acceptance of us.

The Franciscan tradition has a profound respect for the individuality of each person. Francis realized early on that each one of the friars was different, unique—with his own gifts, talents, strengths and weaknesses. That is why both Francis and Clare were very hesitant to legislate specific devotions, fasts and rules. They realized that everyone was not like them. And with the few rules that they did legislate, these two saints always left a deliberate loophole to allow for an exception.

When a particular friar could not maintain the Lenten fast like the other brothers and was calling out in hunger in the middle of the night, Francis got up, prepared a meal and then invited the entire community to table. Francis did not want this one friar to feel embarrassed or guilty for what he physically could not endure.[25] Francis' action is a visible expression of the truest meaning of hospitality: You can be who you are because we are all family here.

To proclaim God as "our" Father in prayer is to proclaim God as "our" Father by the witness of our lives. Practically speaking, that means realizing we are brothers and sisters to one another—and acting accordingly. It means stretching the size of our hearts through compassionate intercession, love and graceful hospitality.

The Family of Creation

Francis of Assisi created space in his heart for *all* creatures—not just human beings. As patron of the environment, he still challenges us to extend compassionate intercession and hospitality to all creation: to treat Brother Air and Sister Earth "courteously," that is, with respect for their integrity and reverence for their existence.

When the friars went to the forest for wood, Francis asked them to be sure to cut the trees so that they would be able to sprout again. He commanded that one part of the vegetable garden be left unplowed so that his sisters, the wildflowers, could go on growing freely. When a brother ran for water to put out the fire which was burning Francis' habit, Francis said, "Brother, do not harm Brother Fire."[26]

As the world continues to shrink to a global village, Francis becomes a symbol of the human heart that is open not just to our brothers and sisters in the flesh but also stretches to include the family of creation: the stars, the

---

[25] The story can be found in Celano's *Second Life* 22, *Omnibus of Sources*, p. 380.
[26] The stories can be found in Celano's *First Life* 60f; *Second Life* 165f; see also *Legend of Perugia* 49-51, *Omnibus of Sources*.

California redwoods, even the smallest of fish swimming in Sister Stream. As a result of such hospitality, Francis rediscovered his rightful place amid the family of creation.

The Garden of Eden

The Garden of Eden is a biblical symbol for the ecological balance and spiritual harmony that God originally intended for creation. From hickory trees to human beings, all of reality formed an elegant tapestry with each created thing an essential thread. Everything was interrelated and interdependent. Intertwined within this original balance and familial harmony was the awareness of God's presence, freely moving about in the "evening breeze" (Genesis 3:8).

The wise stewards of Eden, Adam and Eve, tended this garden with wonder and awe. They saw their Creator reflected in the beautiful tapestry of creation.

But the moment Adam and Eve looked upon that proffered apple with eyes of desire, devoid of original awe, everything changed. "...[T]he woman saw that the tree was... to be desired to make one wise" (Genesis 3:6). They now looked at creation through the glasses of the false self, observing its elements as spokes *for* a wheel, no longer spokes *of* a wheel.

Utility replaced childlike wonder. The mind supplanted the heart. Many descendants of Adam and Eve to this day do not see a tree until they have need of paper.

Of course our utilitarian and pragmatic approach to nature has made miracles that, in days gone by, would have been considered worthy only of God. Irrigation has transformed deserts and wastelands into places of foliage and human habitation. Technology and science have opened up the mysteries of the moon and stars to the human mind.

Computers, satellites, modern communication systems and transportation have helped the community better cope with the tragedies and natural disasters of the world. The wonders of medical science give hope for healing diseases once thought incurable.

Such blessings, however, have cost Mother Earth and her dependents dearly. Pollution on the earth and in the atmosphere have given birth to urban smog and acid rain. Some of God's more fragile creatures have disappeared due to the destruction of natural habitats. Migratory patterns of birds have been upset by industry and construction. The food chain, still the essential provider of daily bread for all creation, is threatened by the synthetic chemicals dumped in rivers, streams and lakes. The false self with its oversized pragmatic hands was an intruder in the Garden of Eden—the original bull in a china shop.

Now, with so much china broken, what are we to do?

The great Franciscan theologian, Saint Bonaventure, saw in Francis a way of rediscovering our right relationship to the things of creation. He portrayed Francis as a New Adam who followed the footprints left behind as God roamed in the "evening breeze." Francis made of creation "a ladder by which he might mount up and embrace Him who is all-desirable."[27]

But how do we rediscover creation as that ladder to God? How do we climb it? Rediscovering creation as a ladder is not something we actively do. Hoping to master the proper technique betrays the blindness of the false self. It simply happens as a result of our contemplation of and hospitality towards creation.

Merton had this experience of walking up the ladder of

---

[27] Saint Bonaventure, *Major Life* 9:1, *Omnibus of Sources*, p. 698.

creation while gazing upon the flowers in the novitiate chapel:

> Beauty of sunlight falling on a tall vase of red and white carnations and green leaves on the altar of the novitiate chapel. The light and dark. The darkness of the fresh, crinkled flower: light, warm and red, all around the darkness. The flower is the same color as blood, but it is in no sense whatever "as red as blood." Not at all! It is as red as a carnation. Only that.
>
> This flower, this light, this moment, this silence: *Dominus est.* Eternity. He passes. He remains. We pass. In and out. He passes. We remain. We are nothing. We are everything. He is in us. He is gone from us. He is not here. We are here in Him.[28]

When we gaze upon the majesty of creation with the original wonder and awe of Adam and Eve, we are pulled out of the utilitarian self-centeredness of the false self and led into the presence of God in which we dwell and which dwells within us. "*Dominus est.* He is in us.... We are here in Him." Contemplative reverence for creation is one of the many roads leading us home to the true self. A true Christian environmentalist, therefore, champions a form of hospitality towards creation: making room for nature and allowing it to be what it is. Only then can we be who we are, as well.

Creatures like giraffes and turnips, in being what the Creator intended them to be, offer God glory and provide a reminder: The more a creature is what God intends it to be, the more it is its true self. Thus, in his sermon to the birds, Merton said: "Esteemed friends, birds of noble lineage, I have no message to you except this: be what you are: be *birds*. Thus you will be your own sermon to yourselves!"[29]

---

[28] Merton, *Conjectures of a Guilty Bystander*, pp. 146-147.
[29] Thomas Merton, *Day of a Stranger*, ed. Robert E. Daggy (Salt Lake City: Gibbs M. Smith, 1981), p. 51.

When rabbits were busily eating all the vegetables in Gethsemani's garden, Merton wrote:

> You have to leave the rabbits what they are, rabbits; and if you just see that they are rabbits you suddenly see that they are transparent, and that the *rabbitness* of God is shining through in all these darn rabbits.

And he quickly added, "And that people are transparent, and that the humanity of God is transparent in people."[30] The more something is its true self, the more it points to the hands of its Creator, the more it becomes a reflection of the Divine. Creation mirrors God like a Wisconsin lake reflecting the sunset. Francis sings of Brother Sun in the Canticle of Creatures, "He bears a likeness of you, Most High One."

Creation's reflection of Divinity does not mean we cannot use creation for our own needs. Creation is, after all, God's gift to us: "See, I have given you every plant yielding seed that is upon the face of all the earth,... you shall have them for food" (Genesis 1:29). Even Francis mentions in his Canticle that Sister Water "is very useful."

But "use" does not imply "abuse." Stewardship means we respect creation for what it is: a gift, a ladder, an intricate tapestry in which we ourselves are woven. We respect its integrity. We don't unravel the threads.

Our chaste respect and use of creation are founded on the fact that creation is a ladder leading to God. Creator and creation are in such a close relationship that a person cannot grab for one without violating the other. To abuse Sister Water is to shatter a precious reflection of God. To ignore the Creator is to be sucked into the black hole of pragmatism from which light never emerges. The false self divides creature from Creator. The true self honors that relationship.

[30] Thomas Merton, "A Life Free from Care," *Cistercian Studies* 3:4 (1970), p. 223.

Thomas Merton once personified creation and gave it this voice:

> You can use me, and God our Father created me that I might be used by you.... But in order to perceive my goodness, you must respect my dignity as a creature of God. If you seek to deflower the pure integrity of my being, and take me to yourself as if I could be fully possessed by you, you will destroy me, and the beauty God has placed in me will vanish out of your hands. Then you will have profited in no way, you will lose me and defile your own soul. But if you respect me, and leave me as I am, and do not seek to seize me with a full and selfish possession, then I will bring you joy.[31]

Such chaste joy recovers the original stance of Adam and Eve in Paradise: wonder and awe. It is sad that contemporary society considers such emotions of the heart useless and impractical. An attempt to save an endangered owl from another suburban residential community can be an expression of hospitality for the wider family of creation. It can be wonder and awe enfleshed in a respect for creation. When such apparently useless acts arise from a compassionate, familial heart, they can help us climb creation's ladder and experience the wise "owl-ness" of God.

The Wolf of Gubbio

According to the *Little Flowers of Saint Francis*, the town of Gubbio was haunted by a large and fierce wolf who devoured both its animals and its citizens. So petrified were the citizens that when they journeyed beyond the walls of the town, they armed themselves "as if they were going to war."

When Francis visited Gubbio, he "took pity on the

---

[31] Merton, *The Silent Life*, p. 28.

people" and decided to confront the beast. Hoping in the Lord Jesus Christ "who is master of all creatures," the saint armed himself not with shield or helmet but with the Sign of the Cross. And the *Little Flowers* continues, "...with his very great faith St. Francis bravely went out to meet the wolf."

The wolf, spying the saint in his territory, charged with mouth wide open. Francis stopped the beast with the Sign of the Cross and immediately acknowledged his relationship to the wolf: "Come to me, Brother Wolf. In the name of Christ, I order you not to hurt me or anyone." Then, as the animal lay at the feet of Francis, the saint declared:

> Brother Wolf, you have done great harm in this region, and you have committed horrible crimes by destroying God's creatures without any mercy. You have been destroying not only irrational animals, but you even have the more detestable brazenness to kill and devour human beings made in the image of God. You therefore deserve to be put to death just like the worst robber and murderer. Consequently everyone is right in crying out against you and complaining, and this whole town is your enemy. But, Brother Wolf, I want to make peace between you and them, so that they will not be harmed by you any more, and after they have forgiven you all your past crimes, neither humans nor dogs will pursue you any more.[32]

The wolf agreed to the peace initiative. As a result, the saint promised that the citizens of Gubbio would feed the animal every day "for I know that whatever evil you have been doing was done because of the urge of hunger." The pact was sealed by hand and paw. Thereupon Francis and the wolf, "like a very gentle lamb," went to the marketplace of the town where the terms of the pact were again publicly stated and accepted. Francis pledged himself as bondsman for the beast.

---

[32] *Little Flowers of St. Francis* 21, *Omnibus of Sources*, p. 1349.

The story concludes like this:

> From that day, the wolf and the people kept the pact which
> St. Francis made. The wolf lived two years more, and it went
> from door to door for food. It hurt no one, and no one hurt
> it. The people fed it courteously. And it is a striking fact that
> not a single dog ever barked at it.
>   Then the wolf grew old and died. And the people were
> sorry, because whenever it went through the town, its
> peaceful kindness and patience reminded them of the virtues
> and the holiness of St. Francis.[33]

The story of the taming of the wolf of Gubbio brings
together many of the themes of this chapter. It is a myth
about rediscovering the harmonious balance and familial
relationships in the Garden of Eden, a land where a son of
Adam could call a wolf "Brother." Prompted by the saint's
compassion, the miracle highlights the transforming power
of love and intercession. It shows how even the most savage
and untamed of beasts can become fraternal and downright
endearing, "like a very gentle lamb."

The story also recognizes that wolves will be wolves;
hunger was the reason for Brother Wolf's crime. So Francis
creatively restored the wolf to a more familial balance in the
food chain. In the end, this tale shows how reverence and
respect can restore dignity to a creature as mangy as a wolf.
And in regaining his dignity, Brother Wolf became a ladder
leading the townspeople of Gubbio to the holiness of God.

Whether it is the first chirp of a sparrow emerging from
his egg or the stunned cry of an infant thrust from the
warmth of the womb, each is a deliberate and essential note
in the larger symphony of creation. We can only enjoy this
music if we are hospitable: if we make space for all our
brothers and sisters, both rational and irrational, and if we

---

[33] Ibid., p. 1351.

allow them to be who they are. As a person gets closer and closer to home, the true self begins to recognize a welcoming song in the Canada geese, in an early afternoon rainbow, in the inactive volcano and in a confused foreigner asking for directions.

Points for Reflection

Do I allow the sins of prejudice and discrimination to tear apart the family of humanity? Against whom? Why am I "so different" from them?

What have my relationships with others taught me about my true self?

Do I pray for others in order to change God's mind or to express my relationship *with* the family of humanity?

Do I take seriously my obligation to stay in touch with current events and to intercede for the problems of the world (famine, war, poverty, unemployment, racial injustice, incurable disease, etc.)?

Has my suffering hardened my heart or made it more compassionate?

Is my spiritual center rooted in the interior law of the heart or in the external law of the commandments?

How do I express a contemplative reverence for the

integrity of creation in my everyday life? Has my use of creation become an abuse?

CHAPTER THREE

'Who Art in Heaven'

My United Airlines flight was approaching Tokyo's Narita Airport. It was a clear, beautiful morning. I nonchalantly looked out of the left side of the plane and there it was: Mount Fuji!

Wide-opened eyes filled with wonder. My heart focused in silent awe. A touch of heaven on earth, I thought, a masterpiece of God. My interior being moved towards adoration: "All praise be yours, my Lord."

And then I chuckled, filled with awe.

All my life I had had a curious fascination for photographs and pictures of Mount Fuji—its mysterious beauty, its snowcapped grandeur. But my experience of Mount Fuji showed me immediately how far off the mark the photographers and artists had been.

Perhaps of all created reality, nothing points more directly to the transcendence of God than mountains. No wonder they are a frequent symbol in spiritual and mystical literature. In primitive societies mountains were always believed to be the home of the gods.

Within our own Judeo-Christian tradition, Mount Sinai was the place where the glory of the Lord settled (Exodus 24:16) and where God gave Moses the Ten Commandments (Exodus 19:16-25). Mount Tabor was the mountain of Jesus' transfiguration (Mark 9:2-8). The Mount of Olives was the place of Jesus' betrayal (Matthew 26:30). In the Letter to the Hebrews, the beautiful eschatological image of Mount Zion is called the "city of the living God" where Jesus, the angels and the souls of the just made perfect are all gathered together (12:22-24). By their very nature, mountains proclaim the awesome and tremendous power of God, the "other worldliness" of the Divine, the fact that we have a Father "who lives in heaven."

When we locate the presence of God "in heaven" in the Lord's Prayer, we are admitting the totally incomprehensible nature of the Divine presence. Quoting from the First Letter of Timothy (6:16), Francis says that God "dwells in light inaccessible."[34] And in his First Rule, Francis says that God is the One "without beginning and without end, he is unchangeable, invisible, indescribable and ineffable, incomprehensible, unfathomable, blessed and worthy of all praise, glorious, exalted, sublime, most high...."[35]

Our words and images stagger, wobble and stumble. No word or image can accurately describe this ineffable, unfathomable and incomprehensible God who lives "in heaven." Our presumptuous attempts to name or describe God end in frustration. *The Cloud of Unknowing* says, "God can be loved. God cannot be thought." For the epigraph of his fifth book of poetry, *The Tears of the Blind Lions*, Merton quotes these words of Léon Bloy, "When those who love God try to talk about Him, their words are blind lions looking for springs in the desert."

Not having had a father for most of my life, I am deeply attracted to the image of God as Abba. But I have to continually remind myself that God is so much more than what the word *father* signifies. That image does not

[34] Admonition 1, *Omnibus of Sources*, p. 78.
[35] Ibid., Rule of 1221, 23, p. 52.

encompass the totality of the Divine reality.

It is like saying, "Eddie is a musician." It might put me in the ballpark. It points like an arrow in a particular direction—but that's it! It does not really tell me who Eddie is. Nor does it describe exactly what he does since Eddie is also a friend and a priest.

In the same way, God is Father. But God is also Mother. Neither of these parental metaphors says everything there is to say about the nature of Divinity. They focus our attention on just one Divine trait and, as a result, can distort the Divine nature. Like the seven blind men who each touched a different part of the elephant's body and then thought their particular description of the animal was adequate, we think our images for God describe the reality of the Divine. But they don't. As a matter of fact, when we think we have discovered the perfect image for God, we have actually discovered the donkey's hitching post. I suspect we shall all want to laugh in awe when we meet God face to face, like I did on seeing Mount Fuji in person.

Just as the elephant is not just the tusk, the tail or the floppy ears, so God is not just Father or Mother—or any one image. Therefore the negation of any image of God is also very true. In the words of Meister Eckhart, "Only the hand that erases can write the true thing about God." In the end, language is both a straitjacket and a mirage before the Divine presence.

Idolatry

In the opening stanzas of his poem "Theory of Prayer," Thomas Merton addresses the inability of human language and art to express God's elusive nature:

Not in the streets, not in the white streets

Nor in the crowded porticoes
Shall we catch You in our words,
Or lock You in the lenses of our cameras,
You Who escaped the subtle Aristotle,
Blinding us by Your evidence,
Your too clear evidence, Your everywhere.

...For the things that we utter turn and betray us,
Writing the names of our sins on flesh and bone
In lights as hard as diamonds.
And the things we think have sold us to the enemy
Writing the names of our sins on the raw marrow
In lights as sharp as glass....[36]

The moment we think we have captured God in an image, metaphor or description, then "the things that we utter turn and betray us." We become idolaters like the ancient Israelites.

In Exodus 32 the Israelites worship a golden calf. Some Scripture scholars have suggested that the sin here is not worship of a man-made object but in thinking that the reality of Yahweh could be contained in something built of human hands:

He took the gold from them, formed it in a mold, and cast an image of a calf; and they said, "These are your gods, O Israel, who brought you up out of the land of Egypt!" (Exodus 32:4)

God refuses to become an object which can be contained by the human mind—whether that's a gold calf or a literary image. God lives in heaven! God dwells in light inaccessible. God is indescribable, ineffable, unfathomable, incomprehensible. God is like the air we breathe: We can never grasp it in our hands. God is like the horizon: We can never take in its length in one single glance. God is like the universe with its black holes and quasars: We will never

---

[36] Merton, "Theory of Prayer," in *The Collected Poems of Thomas Merton*, pp. 179-180.

comprehend it. Indeed, it is an arrogant presumption on the part of the false self to think that God can be captured, photographed, contained or described. God is God: totally other, totally transcendent. As Merton aptly addressed God, "Your everywhere."

In a very rare description of his own prayer, Merton confessed to Abdul Aziz, a Sufi scholar with whom he had been corresponding, that he never imagined or conceived a precise image of God during his personal prayer, "for to my mind this would be a kind of idolatry." Merton continued, "On the contrary, [my prayer] is a matter of adoring Him as invisible and infinitely beyond our comprehension, and realizing Him as all."[37]

Merton once defined idolatry as taking some external sign, object or concept and making it an absolute around which a person's entire spiritual energy is devoted and consecrated. This replaces Divine reality. It becomes an end in itself. The object or sign thus becomes an opaque glass which cannot be penetrated rather than, as it should be, a window into a deeper reality.[38]

Poverty of Spirit

Meister Eckhart once wrote, "It is possible to be 'so poor' that one does not even 'have a God.'" What he meant is that the poor in spirit have abandoned all mental images of God. When the poor in spirit pray, they consistently renounce any image or metaphor because they, like Merton, want to avoid

---

[37] Thomas Merton, letter to Abdul Aziz, dated January 2, 1966, in *The Hidden Ground of Love. The Letters of Thomas Merton on Religious Experience and Social Concerns*, ed. William H. Shannon (New York: Farrar, Straus & Giroux, 1985), p. 63-64.

[38] Thomas Merton, "St. Augustine" (Kansas City, Mo.: Credence Cassettes),tape AA 2236.

all temptation towards idolatry.

Such a stance in the life of prayer reveals a profound realism and poverty. It constantly smashes the golden calves in which the false self attempts to contain the living God.

Though language is crippled before the reality of the Divine, it does have its place. As Merton says: "God rises out of the sea like a treasure in the waves, and when language recedes his brightness remains on the shores of our own being."[39] Words, images and metaphors point in the direction of home, to the interior shore where God dwells. Yet, like the tide which recedes once it washes ashore, my images and descriptions for God should recede so I can fully experience the Divine presence left behind. Only with the "poverty" of awe-filled silence and an empty mind can I truly experience the treasure which already shines brightly within me.

The transcendent God who lives "in heaven" is the God of the Christian, the Jew, the Moslem. These three great world religions all share the same one God and have a deep respect for Divine transcendence. I remember watching Moslems in Cameroon, West Africa, as they pulled out their prayer mats, faced Mecca and began their prostrations and prayers to Allah. Moslems have a tremendous awareness of Allah's presence in their lives and a deep respect for his transcendence—and they publicly call that to mind several times a day.

But it was while visiting a patient named Iridizo in the hospital run by the Franciscan sisters in the village of Shisong that I also realized the great difference between Christianity and Islam.

Black Moslem Iridizo had a lot of questions to ask the

[39] Thomas Merton, *Thoughts in Solitude* (New York: Farrar, Straus, and Cudahy, 1958), p. 86.

visiting white priest from faraway America: "Is it really true that in your country you have machines that make the air in buildings cold? Why would you ever want to do that? And why do you need so many different kinds of cars?"

After we discussed everything from air-conditioning to the American fascination with the automobile, our conversation inevitably turned to the thorny topic of religion. I was surprised at Iridizo's directness: "When we Moslems get together to pray, we are very respectful towards Allah. We pray on special mats. We kneel and bow. We love Allah dearly and we show that by the way we pray. But you Catholics are so different. I went to one of your services and was shocked to see people turning around and shaking hands. How do you show reverence and respect for the Great Compassionate One when everyone is shaking hands?"

Iridizo's question heightened the fundamental difference between Moslems and Christians. For Moslems, Allah lives in heaven and must be shown respect and reverence. For those who profess faith in Jesus, however, the transcendent God who lives in heaven has, in the words of the Fourth Gospel, "become flesh and lived among us" (John 1:14). This is the great Christian insight: The God of the heavens has come down to earth in human flesh. Incarnation!

In the miracle of Christmas, God entered the one thing that *can* contain ineffable Divine reality: the tabernacle of human flesh. To borrow the imagery from Saint Paul, there is a precious treasure found in the clay vessel of human flesh (see 2 Corinthians 4:7).

God's embrace of the body at Christmas and at Jesus' resurrection on Easter morning are two dramatic events which radically affirm the goodness and sanctity of human flesh. Traditional piety has often attempted to evade Paul's challenging reminder, "...[D]o you not know that your body is a temple of the Holy Spirit within you?" (1 Corinthians 6:19).Unfortunately, some Christians still look at flesh and blood as instruments of the devil and threats to a person's spiritual life.

When the God who lives in heaven became the God of human flesh, the enspirited flesh of every human being was consecrated and sacramentalized. As Merton writes:

> For in becoming man, God became not only Jesus Christ but also potentially every man and woman that ever existed. In Christ, God became not only "this" man, but also, in a broader and more mystical sense, yet no less truly, "every man."[40]

The Sacrament of My Neighbor

Because our Father who lives in heaven has taken on flesh and blood, we Christians are challenged to adopt a deeply contemplative vision of each other. We are called to look beyond the superficial appearances of makeup and hairstyles, to see and reverence in our neighbor another dwelling place for the Divine, another temple of the Holy Spirit, another Incarnation.

Yuri Gagarin was the first Soviet cosmonaut to orbit the earth in 1961. Upon his return, he held a news conference in which he arrogantly proclaimed, "Comrades, I have circled far above the earth and have discovered that there is no God in heaven." The story goes that a Russian Orthodox priest immediately stood up and said, "Sir, you will never find God in heaven unless you first find God here on earth."

That is the great test of spirituality for our times. I failed the test on Good Friday 1981.

I had just finished shopping at Hermann's Sporting

[40] Merton, *New Seeds of Contemplation*, pp. 294-295.

Goods in downtown Chicago. Since it was getting near one o'clock, the time the Good Friday Service was to begin, I would have to walk fast to get to the church on time. As I left the store and started down the street, a beggar approached me for a handout. "Hey, Mister, how about a quarter for some food? I haven't eaten in two days." I could tell by the alcohol on his breath that he was telling me only a half-truth. I pretended not to notice him and quickly stepped up my pace. After all, I had to get to church on time.

But after I had walked about thirty yards, something told me to turn around. I looked over my shoulder and froze in my tracks. There was Jesus standing where the beggar had been. And though the street was crowded and I was thirty yards away, I heard Jesus whisper ever so clearly, "Albert, you couldn't give me a quarter? Not even today—on Good Friday?"

On Good Friday 1981 I encountered God in the flesh and I failed the test. To confine God to an image or metaphor is idolatry; to ignore God in my neighbor is blasphemy.

A whole tradition of spirituality emphasizes the need to become aware of the sacrament of my neighbor. Martin of Tours gave half his cloak to a beggar who, that same night, appeared to the saint in a dream as Christ himself. Benedict of Nursia begins chapter 53 of his Rule, "The Reception of Guests," with the unequivocal declaration: "All guests who present themselves are to be welcomed as Christ, for he himself will say: 'I was a stranger and you welcomed me.'"

Augustine of Hippo says, "Do not grieve or complain that you were born in a time when you can no longer see God in the flesh. He did not in fact take this privilege from you. As he says, 'Whatever you have done to the least of my brothers, you did to me.'" Bonaventure suggests that Francis of Assisi's early ministry to the lepers was a direct result of the saint's devotion to the Crucified Christ who was often portrayed in medieval art as a leper.[41] A fourteenth-century text quotes Francis as referring to the lepers as "my Christian brothers" which, for the saint, was equivalent to "my brothers in Christ."[42] In an essay on love, Merton wrote explicitly:

> Any prisoner, any starving man, any sick or dying man, any sinner, any man whatever, is to be regarded as Christ—this is the formal command of the Savior Himself.... Our faith is given us not to see *whether or not* our neighbor is Christ, but to recognize Christ in him and to help our love make both him and ourselves more fully Christ.[43]

Surprisingly, the Christian Scriptures appear eager to highlight the many times that Christ has not been recognized. Matthew bases the final eschatological judgment upon the recognition of Christ in the poor and needy: "[F]or I was hungry and you gave me no food..." (25:42-46). At the tomb on Easter morning, Mary meets the Risen Christ and mistakes him for a gardener (John 20:11-18). The two disciples on the road to Emmaus take the Risen Christ to be an uninformed stranger (Luke 24:13-35). And then there is the case of Saul:

> "Saul, Saul, why do you persecute me?" He asked, "Who are you, Lord?" The reply came, "I am Jesus, whom you are persecuting." (Acts 9:4-5)

The Annunciations of Daily Life

Hasidic Jews believe that angels enter our lives one hundred times a day. Each day, they say, each of us experiences one hundred messengers of the Divine.

---

[41] *Major Life* 1:6, *Omnibus of Sources*, p. 639.
[42] Ibid., *Mirror of Perfection* 58, p. 1184.
[43] Thomas Merton, "The Power and Meaning of Love," in *Disputed Questions* (New York: Farrar, Straus & Giroux, 1960), pp. 124-125.

From this Hasidic point of view, the amazing thing is not that the angel Gabriel entered Mary's life, but that Mary recognized this annunciation of God (Luke 1:26-38). Mary was a great contemplative, intensely focused upon each individual who entered her life. She looked beyond the veil of human flesh and offered hospitality to each person as a messenger of the Divine. She was a woman totally aware that everyone she encountered was a God-bearer. Like the Indian painter Jamini Roy, she believed, "Everyone who comes to my house brings God into it." Like a Zen master, she was wide awake. She was living in the present. From such a stance, she discovered the annunciations of daily life, the epiphany of the now, the sacrament of her neighbors.

During my first year of ministry as a deacon at St. Jude's Parish, New Lenox, Illinois, my frustration must have been quite evident. Most professional ministers learn sooner or later that the primary focus of ministry is people, not paper. But that was a hard lesson for me.

I remember Sister Marcia asking me how I was adjusting to ministerial life "in the real world." I told her it was much tougher than I would have ever imagined. I complained how every time I sat in my office to begin working on the Sunday homily or my adult education presentation, inevitably the phone rang, someone knocked at my door, or I got sidetracked with somebody needing something. I didn't ever seem to make any headway with all the stuff piling up on my desk.

Marcia's response was downright practical. "Remember, Albert, God never makes an appointment!"

Incarnation is not only the basic Christian insight but also the basic ministerial priority. The God who lives in heaven has taken on human flesh. And that God has the terrible habit of always being inconvenient.

Annunciations occur when we least expect them. We all need to heed Meister Eckhart's advice to a sinner who asked for a way to make up for lost time in the spiritual life: "Be in all things a God-seeker and at all times a God-finder, among all kinds of people and in all kinds of circumstances."

Amnesia of the Present

To be a God-seeker demands that we be awake and alert to the here and now. Tragically, many of us suffer from what Merton calls "amnesia of the present."[44]

Many people have lost touch with the present moment because they prefer to live in the past. They are forever mulling over yesterday—either regretting it, analyzing it or glorifying it with nostalgia. Sentimentality, regret and guilt are the prices we pay when the false self lives yesterday today.

Other people are always jumping ahead to the future: anxious about next weekend, planning next month, wondering about next year. With antacids in their pockets and ulcers in their stomachs, they race towards tomorrow! Anxiety and worry are the prices we pay when the false self lives tomorrow today.

Anthony DeMello, S.J., compared our daily predicament to that of a person who, at the very beginning of the symphony, suddenly realizes he has locked his car keys in the automobile. Anxiety divides the person's awareness and freezes him in a semiconscious state. He is unable to enjoy the music unfolding before him because his worry has returned him to the parking lot. He is filled with regret. He is also worried about what will happen after the concert. Who

---

[44] Merton, *New Seeds of Contemplation*, p. 106.

will he call? How much will it cost? The person is stuck, straddling the moment: unable to enjoy the present; unable to fix the past; unable to hasten the future.

Influenced by his study of Zen, Merton came to a deep appreciation for the importance of the present moment:

> Reality is the admission of presence. We make reality in so far as we consent to be present in a situation, that is to say, fully present in a situation... The reason why this particular situation is real is that we are all here. This is what makes it not only a real situation but a *saving* situation....[45]

Later in the same lecture, Merton stated that much suffering originates in our lack of attention to the present. Convinced that the real action is "someplace else," we rarely experience just this particular moment, pregnant with its own annunciations. We are not where we really are. And so, like the man at the symphony, we can't enjoy the music that surrounds us.

The Sacrament of the Here and Now

Our schizophrenic existence of being in one place and wanting to be in another is aided and abetted by our traditional dichotomy between the secular and the sacred, the natural and the supernatural. This Western dualistic thinking can lead to the view that God must be elsewhere since nothing worthy of the Divine can be found in the ordinary, present moment. As Merton notes:

> ...we tend to think that nothing in man's ordinary life is really supernatural except saying prayers and performing pious acts of one sort or another, pious acts which derive their value precisely from the fact that they rescue us,

[45] Thomas Merton, "Solitude and Resurrection" (Kansas City, Mo.: Credence Cassettes), tape AA 2100.

momentarily, from the ordinary routine of life.[46]

Dualistic thinking belittles "the ordinary routine of life," sometimes offering a false sense of control and security. By dividing, categorizing and compartmentalizing, it makes reality seem manageable. Everything becomes ordered. Everything has its determined place. "God is up there. I am down here. Yesterday I did that. Tomorrow I will do this." The false self can then sit back as a proud master and gaze upon the castle it has built with fine theoretical distinctions.

But this house of cards collapses when confronted with the Incarnation. Finely ordered distinctions cannot make sense of the awesome reality of God-made-flesh, of Divinity-on-earth. The Incarnation frustrates the thinking process of the false self by revealing the sacred in the secular, the godlike self, Christ in us. The pig pen of the mind suddenly becomes a burden, and one is challenged to start the journey back home to the sacrament of the here and now.

Merton's own journey as a contemplative witnesses to the integration which occurs as a person returns home. Monastery and world come into dialogue. Spirit and flesh are equally respected. Humanity is experienced as a sacrament of the Divine. Christian spiritual maturity begins when the wall dividing the sacred from the secular comes down. Or to put it more accurately, when one realizes there is no wall in the first place! Explaining his occasional displeasure with mystical literature that is "completely out of touch with ordinary life," Merton wrote in a letter to John C. H. Wu, "mysticism flourishes most purely right in the middle of the ordinary."[47]

While in mainland China in 1991, I had a Chinese

[46] Merton, *Conjectures of a Guilty Bystander*, p. 81.
[47] Merton, letter to John C. H. Wu, dated December 12, 1961, in *The Hidden Ground of Love*, pp. 620-621.

calligrapher make a scroll bearing an oft-repeated dictum of my Zen teacher: "After enlightenment, do the laundry." A more accurate rendering of the teaching would have been, "Enlightenment is doing the laundry." Or perhaps the most accurate, "Do laundry."

To return home is to return to the sacrament of the here and now where Abba waits. It is to break through the lie of dualism with its schizophrenic anxiety. It is to experience union with God, the godlike self, Christ in us. This experience is a rediscovery of what is *within*: "[I]t is no longer I who live, but it is Christ who lives in me" (Galatians 2:20). It is also a rediscovery of what is *without*: "In [God] we live and move and have our being" (Acts 17:28a).

To be precise, there is no "within" or "without." There is only Christ, the "fullness of him who fills all in all" (Ephesians 1:23). No wonder Catherine of Siena could state unabashedly, "All the way to heaven is heaven."

'Nothing Left to Do'

Like the prodigal son, some people lose sight of what they already have and wander off. They then turn the journey home, the awareness of being rooted in God, into a project, a task, a hobby. In a very pragmatic way, they set out with tackle box and bait in the confident hope of reeling in God. They develop strategies and techniques. They talk about degrees and distinguish stages as bench marks of progress. But this approach, steeped in the dualism of the false self, completely misses the most obvious reality: We already have what we desperately want.

In one of his Sunday afternoon lectures to the monks of Gethsemani, Merton said that real spiritual growth simply means being more deeply centered "in one's own reality—

one's own rootedness which is God." Such a reality is "too simple, too near and too real." He continued:

> Because it's so simple, we complicate it in order to have something to do. We invent all these funny ways of talking about the thing and then it gets to be a great project and you get lost in this project and forget the simple reality which is always there.[48]

To beat a dead horse: The graced union between God and a human being is completely natural and already present. It is what makes us who we are right now. We simply need to become aware of it. We simply need to come back home or, as Merton put it, to find "the happiness of being at one with everything in that hidden ground of Love for which there can be no explanations."[49]

Union with "that hidden ground of Love" is presented in John's Gospel as Jesus' final prayer and legacy to his disciples: "I pray, Abba, that the love with which you loved me may be in them" (see John 17:20-26). It is the constitutive reality of human existence. As the fifteenth-century married saint, Catherine of Genoa, exclaimed from her own experience, "My *me* is God!" A person does not go in search of that union. One simply needs to become conscious of what one already has. Merton describes that realization with a startling paradox:

> In a Zen koan someone said that an enlightened man is not one who seeks Buddha or finds Buddha, but simply an ordinary man *who has nothing left to do*. Yet mere stopping is not arriving. To stop is to stay a million miles from it and to do nothing is to miss it by the whole width of the universe. As for arriving, when you arrive you are ruined. Yet how

[48] Thomas Merton, "Spiritual Direction" (Kansas City, Mo.: Credence Cassettes), tape AA 2137.
[49] Merton, letter to Amiya Chakravarty, dated April 13, 1967, in *The Hidden Ground of Love*, p. 115.

close the solution is: how simple it would be to have nothing more to do if only—one had really nothing more to do. The man who is unripe cannot get there, no matter what he does or does not do. But the ripe fruit falls out of the tree without even thinking about it. Why? The man who is ripe discovers that there was never anything to be done from the very beginning.[50]

Christian mystics and Zen masters have continually reminded us that, from the beginning, all is one. Original unity. The mysticism of the ordinary. The sacrament of the present moment. There is nothing to get somewhere else because we already have it right here. Indeed, there's no place like home. As a matter of fact, there's no place *but* home.

Points for Reflection

Am I so invested in my images for God that I commit idolatry, confusing the image for the reality? Do I find it difficult to let go of them and open myself up to Eckhart's "poverty of spirit"?

Do I have an authentically contemplative vision that sees in my neighbor a sacred vessel of Divinity? Am I sensitive to the annunciations occurring in my everyday routine?

Do I suffer from "amnesia of the present," always living in the past or future? Why do I shy away from the experience of the present moment?

[50] Merton, *Conjectures of a Guilty Bystander*, p. 258.

When do I experience my union with Merton's "hidden ground of Love"?

CHAPTER FOUR

'Hallowed Be Thy Name'

I was named "Albert" after my grandfather. Within hours after my baptism, however, an elderly Ursuline nun pronounced my name in her native French: "Al-bear"—with no "t" pronounced. It was a smash hit! "So unique, so different," the shoe salesman of Russian descent and his wife thought. So my parents decided to adopt the French pronunciation.

Growing up, I developed a "thing" about my name. I liked the way it sounded. It set me apart. It also had an air of sophistication that occasionally fed my false self. And it's been the source of a laugh or two. When I first introduce myself, people often reply, "Nice to meet you, Father Al." And I always have to tell them, "No. It's Father *Al-bear*—like 'Teddy Bear.'" I've stopped counting the number of letters I've received addressed to "Father Al Bear." Ah, the price of sophistication!

Names are precious and sacred. Indeed, a person's relationship to us is expressed in the name he or she calls us. A name can throb with intimacy when used by someone who loves us. (My mother is the only person on earth who can get away with calling me her "Sugar Pie.") Or a name can be a formal means of address replete with all appropriate honor and respect. ("Mrs. Jones," "Archbishop Lyke," "Your Holiness.")

People sometimes ask our permission to address us in a personal way. The first question my new eye doctor asked me was, "Father, may I call you by your first name?" I am sometimes a bit surprised when someone I have never met before just presumes that level of intimacy, for names are special. They should be permitted to suggest and express the appropriate level of familiarity, depth of relationship and the intensity of intimacy.

According to the Hebrew Scriptures, name and existence are closely associated. To have no name is to have no existence in reality. To have a name is to have an existence. And to know a name is to have knowledge and a relationship with that person.

With this in mind, we can see how the use of the different names of God at different points in time suggest a closer and closer relationship between God and God's people. As God gets closer to the chosen people, God reveals more and more of the Divine identity in the holy name. Intimacy is expressed through knowledge of the name.

Up to the time of Abraham, God is known as "Elohim." But to the patriarchs God is known by the obscure title "El Shaddai."

God revealed to Moses a new name. It was considered so sacred that the Jews never wrote the new name in full. They wrote only its four consonants, "YHWH"; thus it was never pronounced. They substituted the more distant "Adonai" in public reading.

The revelation of this Divine name occurred at the burning bush in Exodus 3. Merton calls it "one of the most important texts in the Bible."[51]

---

[51] Thomas Merton, *Seasons of Celebration: Meditations on the Cycle of Liturgical Feasts* (New York: Farrar, Straus & Giroux, 1950),p. 192.

But Moses said to God, "If I come to the Israelites and say to them, 'The God of your ancestors has sent me to you,' and they ask me, 'What is his name?' what shall I say to them?" God said to Moses, "I AM WHO I AM." He said further, "Thus you shall say to the Israelites, 'I AM has sent me to you.'" God also said to Moses, "Thus you shall say to the Israelites, 'The LORD, the God of your ancestors, the God of Abraham, the God of Isaac, and the God of Jacob, has sent me to you:'

This is my name forever,
and this my title for all generations. (3:13-15)

According to the Hebrew mentality, Moses' knowledge of the holy name would serve as proof to the Israelites of his direct experience of this God. And knowledge of the Divine name also meant a relationship.

Jesus also introduced a new name for God: "Abba." This name, suggesting intense intimacy and almost scandalous familiarity, sent shock waves through traditional Judaism. It spoke of a unique relationship with God unparalleled in its time. The scandal of this new name drove the first nail on Good Friday.

From the biblical perspective, the Divine name has a sacramental quality. God is present in the holy name. Every time I say "Abba," I become aware of Abba's presence surrounding me and dwelling within me. Thus I do not say God's name flippantly or absent-mindedly. The Divine name is weighted with the Divine presence. It must be "hallowed"— kept holy.

Francis of Assisi sings in his Canticle of Creatures that God is so glorious that "no one is worthy to mention your name." The first dimension of hallowing the name of God, then, is to recognize God's very presence in the name. That's what we do when we say "hallowed be thy name" in the Lord's Prayer.

The spontaneous response to the presence of God in the

proclamation of the name is awe-filled adoration. I open up my entire being to the God whose unconditional love not only fills the universe in every way but also is the very heart of my existence.

But there is a second—and sobering—dimension to hallowing the Divine name. It means recognizing my own presence and what that means before a loving God. Here arises one of the great paradoxes of the spiritual life.

God, through Jesus, invites me to call him "Abba." Now calling God "Abba" is like meeting the President of the United States and having him say, "Call me Bill." Or meeting the Pope and having him say, "Call me Karol." A tension immediately emerges between feeling unworthy and, at the same time, wanting to accept the invitation to intimacy.

In keeping God's name holy, I experience the paradox between the awe-inspiring presence of God and my awful unworthiness, between the adoration of the Divine presence and the abomination of my sinful presence. Adoration and abomination walk hand-in-hand. This paradox gives birth to the virtue of humility.

Humility

Humility comes from the Latin word *humus* which means "dirt" or "ground." Humility is the virtue that keeps my feet on the ground—even as I come into the Divine presence by presuming to call God "Abba." It is a fruit of self-knowledge. During a Holy Week retreat in 1941, before entering the Trappists, Merton wrote:

> As soon as we know ourselves even a little, we necessarily become humble—or at least we are humbled! As soon as we know ourselves, we know our contingency and our dependence. To know this, to accept this, is to become

humble.... We must long to learn the secret of our own nothingness....[52]

The humility of self-knowledge keeps me from being puffed up with pride. As Saint Francis used to say, "What a man is before God, that he is, and no more."[53] And before God, each one of us stands as an unworthy creature steeped in the insignificance of our own existence. Psalm 8 says it so well:

O LORD, our Sovereign,
how majestic is your name over all the earth!

You have set your glory above the heavens....

When I look at your heavens, the work of your fingers,
the moon and the stars that you have established,
what are human beings that you are mindful of them,
mortals that you care for them? (8:3-4)

To hallow the Divine name is to accept the insignificance of my own existence.

But such humble self-acceptance, if it is to be authentic, must be in communion with reality and truth. Authentic humility faces reality squarely. As *The Cloud of Unknowing* says, "People are humble when they stand in the truth with a knowledge and appreciation for themselves as they really are." True humility is not afraid to acknowledge the certain talents and gifts given by God.

Truly humble people hallow the Divine name by recognizing in the Divine presence who God has created them to be, what gifts and talents God has graciously bestowed upon them, and how God has acted in their lives. In the words of the Virgin Mary, "The Mighty One has done

[52] Thomas Merton, *The Secular Journal of Thomas Merton* (New York: Farrar, Straus & Giroux, 1959),pp. 196-197.
[53] Admonition 20, *Omnibus of Sources*, p. 84.

great things for me, and holy is his Name" (Luke 1:49).

False humility, on the other hand, does not face the truth of my human existence. It claims that God made a mistake when he created me. It promotes a tragic feeling of absolute worthlessness. It is self-contempt. Always putting myself down is just as wrong and just as sinful as always raising myself up!

Authentic humility never degenerates into becoming a "door mat for Jesus," sacrificing all self-respect and self-esteem. As Merton says, "Humility is a virtue, not a neurosis."[54]

False humility is one expression of the false self at work. Pride is another. It takes personal credit for everything: talents, gifts, accomplishments and abilities. It commands an audience for what it perceives to be its own creation. It demands to take a bow and have an encore. The deformed, proud ego claims itself as master and creator. A good way to think of ego is E-G-O: Easing God Out.

Pride, says Francis in his second Admonition, was the original sin of Adam and Eve in the Garden of Paradise. They exalted themselves and took personal credit for the grace of God in their lives. Their egos "eased God out" of Paradise.

True humility puts God back where God belongs. It focuses exclusively upon God and the grace of God at the center of life. True humility is aware—and stunned by—the fullness of God's grace and love everywhere. It is an incarnation of the very holiness of God.

Throughout his twenty-eight Admonitions, Francis continually reminds us that God is the One who does the speaking and acting through us. God is the One who accomplishes all the good in our lives. This realization kept

[54] Merton, *Thoughts in Solitude*, p. 65.

Francis humble. As the saint wrote in the seventeenth chapter of the Rule of 1221, "Let us refer all good to the most high and supreme Lord God and acknowledge that every good is His; let us thank Him for everything, He from Whom all good things come."

Authentic humility lives with the awareness that I am simply an earthen vessel—*humus*—through which the surpassing power of God acts (see 2 Corinthians 4:7). Adoration of the surpassing power of God and the abomination of my earthen vessel are bound together. The awareness of this interplay between grace and nature, between adoration and abomination, is the very ground of Franciscan humility.

One day, Brother Masseo went up to Saint Francis and asked, "Why after you? Why after you? Why after you?"

Saint Francis replied, "What do you mean, Brother Masseo?"

"I mean, why does all the world seem to be running after you, and everyone seems to want to see you and hear you and obey you? You are not a handsome man. You do not have great learning or wisdom. You are not a nobleman. So why is all the world running after you?"

After a moment of prayer, the saint replied:

You really want to know why everyone is running after me? I have this from the all-holy eyes of God that see the good and the evil everywhere. For those blessed and all-holy eyes have not seen among sinners anyone more vile or insufficient than I am. And so in order to do that wonderful work which He intends to do, He did not find on earth a viler creature, and therefore He chose me, for God has chosen the foolish things of the world to put to shame the wise, and God has chosen the base things of the world and the despised, to bring to naught the noble and great and strong, so that all excellence in virtue may be from God and not from the creature, in order that no creature should glory before Him, but "let him who takes pride, take pride in the Lord," that honor and glory may be only God's forever.[55]

A third dimension of hallowing the Divine name is to live with the awareness of the dynamic power of God working through the earthen vessel of my sinful life. To paraphrase Mary's statement in contemporary terms: "God writes straight with my crooked lines and holy is the name!"

The Name of Jesus

Our Christian tradition goes one step further. Not only is God's name holy, so is the very name of our brother and savior, Jesus. This name also effects what it means. In first-century Judaism the name Jesus in Hebrew, "Joshua," literally meant "Yahweh helps." This was often interpreted as "Yahweh saves." Thus the angel tells Joseph that Mary "will bear a son, and you are to name him Jesus, for he will save his people from their sins" (Matthew 1:21).

The early Church recognized the power of Jesus' name. To the crippled man at the Beautiful Gate, Peter said, "I have no silver or gold, but what I have I give you; in the name of Jesus Christ of Nazareth, stand up and walk" (Acts 3:6). The Johannine Jesus invites us to ask for anything in his name (John 16:23). In the Acts of the Apostles 4:10-12, Peter proclaims to the Sanhedrin that it was by the name of Jesus Christ that the crippled man was able to walk.

Peter then concludes with a statement that astonishes his listeners: "There is salvation in no one else, for there is no other name under heaven given among mortals by which we must be saved" (4:12). As the famous Christian hymn in the Letter to the Philippians concludes:

---

[55] *Little Flowers of Saint Francis*, 10, *Omnibus of Sources*, p. 1323.

Therefore God also highly exalted him
  and gave him the name
  that is above every name,
so that at the name of Jesus
  every knee should bend,
  in heaven and on earth and under the earth,
and every tongue should confess
  that Jesus Christ is Lord,
  to the glory of God the Father. (2:9-11)

The name of Jesus has continued to be hallowed by Christians down through the centuries. The Orthodox tradition gave birth to the Jesus Prayer: "Jesus, Son of David, have mercy on me, a sinner." And Orthodox spiritual writers have insisted upon the power inherent in the recitation of the name of Jesus: "The remembrance of the name of God utterly destroys all that is evil" (the two Elders of Gaza, Saints Barsanuphius and John); "Flog your enemies with the name of Jesus for there is no weapon more powerful in heaven or on earth" (Saint John Climacus). Many Orthodox writers believe that the name of Jesus is so sacred, precious and powerful, that it should never be pronounced or prayed by itself. Rather, it should always be watered down with an adjective or an invocation: "Jesus, save me!" "Loving Jesus!" "Jesus, remember me!" From the Orthodox perspective, the intensity and power of the name of Jesus could overwhelm the one who pronounces it unaccompanied by a modifier. In Christian spirituality, this hallowing of Jesus' name has given rise to a way of praying at all times and living continually in the Divine presence.

The Jesus Prayer

The Way of a Pilgrim is a journal of an anonymous nineteenth-century Russian Christian. At the Divine Liturgy on the twenty-fourth Sunday after Pentecost, the Russian heard these words in the day's epistle: "[P]ray without ceasing" (1 Thessalonians 5:17).Curiosity about these words inspired him to wander the steppes of his motherland in search of a method of unceasing prayer.

After a year, this pilgrim arrived at a monastery where an elder taught him the Jesus Prayer. The pilgrim was initially told to limit his recitation of the prayer to three thousand times a day. Then six thousand times a day. Finally, after ten days of laborious recitation, he could increase it to twelve thousand times a day. One day, during this last period of practice, he woke up and what had been previously a labor for him was suddenly second nature. From that moment on, the Jesus Prayer became the constant prayer of his heart.

Recitation of the Divine name changed the pilgrim's relationship with all creation. In the pilgrim's words:

> When I began to pray with the heart, everything around me became transformed and I saw it in a new and delightful way. The trees, the grass, the earth, the air, the light, and everything seemed to be saying to me that it exists to witness to God's love for [all] and that it prays and sings of God's glory.[56]

The name of Jesus opened the pilgrim's eyes so that, like Francis of Assisi, he rediscovered creation's original purpose: the glory and praise of God. The Jesus Prayer moved the pilgrim to a contemplative hospitality towards inanimate objects. Thus all creation became a ladder leading him home, to the awareness of Divine love in the present moment.

The prayer also transformed the pilgrim's relationship to others:

...I spent the rest of the summer reciting the name of Jesus

[56] *The Way of a Pilgrim* and *The Pilgrim Continues His Way*, trans. Helen Bacovcin (Garden City, N.Y.: Image Books, 1978),p. 34.

vocally and I enjoyed great peace. If I happened to meet people during the day they all seemed as close to me as if they were my kinsmen, even though I did not know them.... The calling on the name of Jesus Christ comforted me on the road; all people seemed good to me and I felt that everyone loved me.... When someone offends me, I remember how sweet the Jesus Prayer is and the offense and anger disappear and I forget everything.[57]

The power of the name of Jesus acted as a healing balm for the wounds and divisions among people caused by the selfishness, blindness and prejudice of the false self. The pilgrim was able to look into the eyes of each person he encountered and see his brother or sister. He thus rediscovered the family of humanity.

Thomas Merton liked *The Way of a Pilgrim* and found it to be a "good stimulating book to read." But he expressed a reservation about the traditional practice of the Jesus Prayer: "I think it is all very well for a hard-headed nineteenth-century Russian moujik to do that all day and all night, but it is not going to work for Americans today."[58]

Merton found the repetition of the prayer useful at times, but it was certainly "too much and not necessary" to center one's entire spiritual life upon it. His own practice was minimal and only during dry periods: "when I am plagued with distractions or half dead with sleep and can't do anything better." He believed that the Jesus Prayer was simply a technique that could sometimes help promote attention to the presence of God in one's heart. He wrote to the other monk:

[57] Ibid., pp. 23-24.
[58] Thomas Merton, letter to Father Thomas Fidelis (Francis)Smith, O.C.S.O., dated June 29, 1963, in *The School of Charity. The Letters of Thomas Merton on Religious Renewal and Spiritual Direction*, ed. Brother Patrick Hart (New York: Farrar, Straus, and Giroux, 1990),pp. 176-177.

As for the breathing, I would get some idea of some good
Yoga breathing, as described in a reliable book like
Dechanet's *Christian Yoga*, and use that *sometimes*. But for
the rest, the light of the Lord shines in our hearts always and
all we need to do is to remind ourselves of it in the simplest
possible way, and surrender to Him totally. If a simple
ejaculation helps, well and good. Words do not always help.
Just looking is often more helpful.[59]

Merton was opposed to turning the Jesus Prayer into the
exclusive technique of one's spiritual life, or even worse, into
an end in itself. That would be a form of idolatry. The Jesus
Prayer is one means among many, not necessarily the best
means, and its only function is to make one aware of what
one already has:

It seems to me that the Bible is a much better source of light
than the Jesus Prayer. But all sources fail, except God
Himself. And He is after all the most accessible. We get tired
of means once in a while, and that is perhaps because we are
nearer to the end than we realize.[60]

Spiritual Techniques

Praying the holy name of Jesus should keep me focused
in the sacrament of the present moment. As a matter of fact,
the purpose of any spiritual technique—be it the Jesus
Prayer, Scripture reading, or a step-by-step meditation—is to
make me aware of the presence of God in which I dwell and
that dwells within me. Techniques function only as arrows
which point my attention to the Divine presence. They do
not lead me to a union with God as if that union could be
attained by my own efforts; rather, they make me aware of
the communion with God that I already share as a result of

[59] Ibid.
[60] Ibid.

Divine grace at the center of my being. To use the Zen expression, they are simply "fingers pointing to the moon." They are not to become idols or ends in themselves. Consequently, I should let go of the technique as soon as it has served its purpose: making me aware of what I already have, Divine love. When I find myself distracted or inattentive to the "light of the Lord shining in the heart," to use Merton's expression from his letter on the Jesus Prayer, I return to the technique but only for as long as I need it to consciously awaken me again to the presence of the Divine. Consciously hallowing the Divine presence is hallowing the name.

A silent, loving awareness of God without any conscious reflection or discursive thought is the goal. Merton reminds us:

> Let us never forget that the fruitful silence in which words lose their power and concepts escape our grasp is perhaps the perfection of meditation. We need not fear and become restless when we are no longer able to "make acts." Rather we should rejoice and rest in the luminous darkness of faith. This "resting" is a higher way of prayer.[61]

Once I become aware of the Divine presence through the recitation of God's name, I should leave all thoughts and techniques aside and simply return God's contemplative glance of love. Silent awe is the language of love. It is the adoration of the poor in spirit. Continuing with a technique out of sheer habit or willpower, is to risk spiritual stagnation or even idolatry.

A word of caution is in order. Timing is everything in the spiritual life. Renouncing techniques before a person is mature enough "is useless," Merton told the monks. "The whole business of [spiritual] growth is knowing when to let

---

[61] Merton, *Spiritual Direction and Meditation*, p. 48.

go."[62] And that, of course, is one area in which spiritual direction can be helpful as the directee discerns when to use a technique and when to drop it.

The false self impulsively turns the spiritual life into a project and a task of the ego. But what is the false self trying to get that a person doesn't already have? The false self prays from where it thinks it should be or would like to be. The true self prays from where it is.

Unceasing Prayer

God is like the FM radio music constantly playing in the background of my life. Though I am not always consciously aware of it, the music continues playing. Once in a while a particular melody grabs my conscious attention. Then I stop what I'm doing and hum along with the music. After a few moments, or at the conclusion of the song, I go back to what I was doing. Sometimes my activity—some manual labor or enjoying a cup of tea—can proceed hand-in-hand with my singing for an extended period of time. At these times the activity of the present moment and attention to the background music are bound together in one and the same act.

The experience of unceasing prayer, the traditional goal of the Jesus Prayer, is analogous to my relationship with the FM radio music playing in the background. Periodically, the Divine presence commands my attention. So I stop what I'm doing and momentarily bask in the light of the Lord. Or I continue what I'm doing but with conscious awareness that I'm doing it in the light of the Lord.

My set periods of prayer when I make deliberate use of techniques make me more prayerful, more attuned to the fullness of the Divine presence in which I dwell and that dwells within. They provide the ambiance for unceasing prayer.

As I become more prayerful and contemplative in my stance towards reality, I become more attentive to God's presence in the ordinary routines of everyday life: in creation, in the people whom I encounter, in my solitary moments of waiting, driving, or doing dishes. Thus, unceasing prayer is never dissociated from respect for creation, hospitality towards others, or the sacrament of the present moment.

Finally, there comes a point when my prayerfulness leads to the great secret of the spiritual life: Prayer is not "becoming aware and taking notice of the presence of God in which we dwell and that dwells within"; rather, prayer is the realization that at every moment of my existence Abba is already contemplating me.

This experience of God as the constant *subject*—not object—of prayer is the beginning of unceasing prayer. I forget myself and enter into communion with the very prayer life of God. "...[W]e do not know how to pray as we ought, but that very Spirit intercedes with sighs too deep for words" (Romans 8:26). "Pray in the Spirit at all times in every prayer and supplication" (Ephesians 6:18). As Merton told a group of religious before heading to the East:

> Let Jesus pray. Thank God Jesus is praying. Forget yourself. Enter into the prayer of Jesus. Let him pray in you.... The best way to pray is: stop. Let prayer pray within you.... In the end, Praise praises. Thanksgiving gives thanks. Jesus prays.[63]

---

[63] Steindl-Rast, pp. 87, 89.

Bernardine of Siena

No preacher was more aware of the power of the name of Jesus than the great fifteenth-century Franciscan, Bernardine of Siena. He was a zealous promoter of the veneration of the name of Jesus throughout Italy. In his day, many Italian city-states were torn by different rival factions, each with its own party emblem or logo. As a way of breaking down those divisions and bringing people together, Bernardine made banners emblazoned with the emblem "YHS," the abbreviation of the Greek word for Jesus. He then organized processions behind these banners to symbolize the surpassing of old allegiances, the destruction of all rivalries and the unity that Christians share in the name of Jesus. And so through the power of the holy name as well as Bernardine's creative, one might even say superstitious, maneuvering, many people in rival factions were brought together in unity and peace.

It is most appropriate to conclude this chapter on hallowing the Divine name with words once preached by Bernardine of Siena:

> Glorious name, gracious name, name of love and of power! Through you sins are forgiven, through you enemies are vanquished, through you the sick are freed from their illness, through you those suffering in trials are made strong and cheerful. You bring honor to those who believe, you teach those who preach, you give strength to the toiler, you sustain the weary. Our love for you is ardent and glowing, our prayers are heard; the souls of those who contemplate you are filled to overflowing, and all the blessed in heaven are filled with your glory. Sweet Jesus, grant that with the blessed in heaven we too may reign through this your most holy name. (*On the Eternal Gospel*, Sermon 49)

Points for Reflection

What is my favorite name for God? And what is God's favorite name for me?

Is my humility a fruit of honest self-knowledge or self-contempt?

Has my ego "eased God out" of my life?

Am I gratefully aware of how God acts in my life? Through my life?

Do my spiritual techniques help me to become aware of God's presence in which I dwell and that dwells within me?

Have I ever experienced "unceasing prayer," the experience of God as the subject—not object—of prayer?

CHAPTER FIVE

'Thy Kingdom Come'

I n the Garden of Eden all creation was interrelated and interdependent. Adam and Eve basked in the presence of God. All was one in the reality of Abba's love. "God saw everything that he had made, and indeed, it was good" (Genesis 1:31).

Divine attention riveted upon Adam and Eve. The heart of God, like that of any other captivated parent, began brimming over with hopes, dreams and wishes. Abba so loved and marveled at Adam and Eve that he gave them the greatest gift possible. He placed all creation into their laps and made them its stewards. They were to nurture this world with tender care, all the while preserving it as a place where there would be no war, violence, or distrust; a place where there would be no racism, inequality, or prejudice; and a place where the hearts of creation's family would reach out to one another. Adam and Eve became the awe-filled guardians of God's Dream of peace, justice and love.

Original Sin

But God's Dream was soon transformed into a nightmare. Adam and Eve, by choosing to ignore this Dream, committed the original sin. The false self appeared like lightning, easing God out and pretending to be the lord of creation.

With the entry of this intruder, creation was thrown into disarray and knocked out of balance. Adam and Eve, by failing to keep the Dream, also lost the immediate awareness of God's all-embracing presence and were pushed from their home (Genesis 3:24). God's Dream suddenly became a fuzzy memory.

It became the job of prophets like Isaiah to glimpse God's original Dream and hold it up to a floundering people:

> ...they shall beat their swords into plowshares,
>   and their spears into pruning hooks;
> nation shall not lift up sword against nation,
>   neither shall they learn war any more. (2:4)
>
> The wolf shall live with the lamb,
>   the leopard shall lie down with the kid,
> the calf and the lion and the fatling together,
>   and a little child shall lead them....
> They will not hurt or destroy
>   on all my holy mountain;
> for the earth will be full of the knowledge of the LORD
>   as the waters cover the sea. (11:6, 9)

The Kingdom of God

Jesus enfleshed the Dream. He called it the "Kingdom of God" and in twenty-nine Gospel stories and comparisons taught its essentials about peace, justice and love. The earliest Gospel begins with Jesus proclaiming: "The time is fulfilled, and the kingdom of God has come near; repent, and believe in the good news" (Mark 1:14).

Jesus befriended the social and religious outcasts of his day (Matthew 11:19; Luke 15:1). At the synagogue of Nazareth, he proclaimed his commitment to peace and justice (Luke 4:16-21). He challenged his listeners to forgive and love their enemies (Matthew 6:12, 14-15, 5:43-48).

Jesus told parables, urging his listeners to return home (Luke 15:11-32) and let the Kingdom come into their lives (Matthew 13:1-58). When we followers pray, "Thy Kingdom come!," we call to mind Abba's great Dream for us and how Jesus lived this Kingdom of peace, justice and love.

Remembering is just the beginning, though. Our real challenge is to live the Dream of the Kingdom as well—in our own lives, in our own times. As St. Augustine said, "To pray 'Thy Kingdom come!' is to pray for the grace of living the right way." And the "right way" means keeping God's Dream alive by the witness of our lives.

Abba depends upon the witness of men and women, centered in the godlike self, for the final realization of the Kingdom. Merton writes:

> The world was created without man, but the new creation which is the true Kingdom of God is to be the work of God in and through man. It is to be the great, mysterious, theandric work of the Mystical Christ, the New Adam, in whom all men as "one Person" or one "Son of God" will transfigure the cosmos and offer it resplendent to the Father.[64]

The Dream's realization is therefore a cooperative venture between God and believers, between Divine grace and human life. It emerges and is established as human hearts become hungry and are willing to die for the peace the world cannot give; as they are ready to be broken out of a love that is pure gift; and as they are bold enough to renounce the ego and work for justice. Indeed, the life of the person rooted in the true self is oriented for and by the final coming of the Kingdom.

[64] Merton, *Zen and the Birds of Appetite*, p. 132.

Dream-keepers and Kingdom People

I once met a friar in Rome who had spent some time studying some primitive tribes in Kenya. He told me that one particular tribe had an almost mystical connection to the primal element of fire. During their long rainy season, certain elders of the tribe had been designated as "keepers of the flame." During the driving afternoon rains, these elders had the responsibility of preserving a fire in their huts. Losing the fire was tantamount to losing the heart of the tribe.

In a similar way Christians are called to be "keepers of the Dream." We go through life praying "Thy Kingdom come" and all the while working for it by our witness to peace, justice and love. We must not allow the Dream to be ignored or forgotten. Our task is to preserve the Dream by leaving our pigpens and returning home. Baptism is the commitment by a community—and by individuals—to keep the Dream alive.

Every now and then, we meet or hear of people who keep the Dream alive in a vivid way. People like the prophet Isaiah, Francis of Assisi, Elizabeth Ann Seton, Oscar Romero and many others were rooted in the true self and thus became living incarnations of the Dream. Though the list is far from exhaustive, four personal traits are characteristic of those who witness to the Kingdom and keep the Dream alive: awareness of God's love, love of others, surrender to the present, and peace and joy.

Awareness of God's Love

Before I began teaching fifth-grade religion, I had been warned about Tommy Nicholson. Eleven-year-old Tommy was seen by all as a holy terror. And the more anyone punished him, I was told, the more Tommy would yell, fight and generally turn the classroom into a purgatory for everybody.

The school counselor told me that Tommy was simply trying to get the attention and love that he did not get at home. So I decided to take a different approach with him. I continually showered him, to the point of favoritism, with love, attention and affection.

And guess what? It worked! The school's holy terror was transformed into a guardian angel who not only became the teacher's pet but also a model of conduct for his fifth-grade classmates.

And what was the secret? Love. For the first time in his eleven years of life, Tommy Nicholson knew that he was loved.

The first characteristic of those who keep God's Dream alive and witness to the Kingdom in their lives is: They know in their bones that they are first and foremost the beloved of Abba. And the experience of Divine love grounds them in the present moment. Indeed, it *is* the ground of the present moment. As Thomas Merton once wrote to a friend, one of the most important tasks in the spiritual life is to experience God's love "not as an abstraction, but as a reality, as *the* reality."[65]

The false self's agenda, by pulling us away from the present moment, the family of creation and relationships

[65] Merton, letter to Linda (Parsons) Sabbath, dated January 29, 1966, in *The Hidden Ground of Love*, p. 525.

with others, also pulls us away from Abba's love incarnated in the world around us. Consequently, God's love becomes a theory, an abstraction, something "to believe in." It becomes a "thing to get."

Dream-keepers and Kingdom people, by contrast, live at home, in the sacrament of the present moment. Their lives overflow with awe as they experience life, Divine love, touching them in the family of creation and humanity. Each moment is an annunciation. Each creature is an epiphany of the Divine. Each person is an angel, another reminder of what they already have.

Once I experience Divine love, the wound of my heart stops bleeding and my life changes drastically—just like eleven-year-old Tommy Nicholson's. I no longer have the obsessive need to prove myself, gain the attention of others, or make a name for myself. I no longer have to be perfect, cute or popular. I stop hating myself. I stop fighting against myself. And I begin to lose interest in the selfish concerns of the false self as the first rays of the true self, enlightening the path leading home, shine over the soul's horizon.

Love of Others

The people of God's Dream have hearts like Abba's: big, tender and exceptionally compassionate. The beloved of God are impelled to become lovers of others. They accept others, respect them, and sometimes even love them. Dream-keepers know that we are all one family with the same Father. They know that most people are doing the best they can, so there is no need to be overly critical, hateful or insensitive. Unconditional acceptance of others reveals the depths of one's own self-acceptance; love of others reveals one's personal capacity to accept Abba's love.

Acceptance of others, hospitality and love are the signatures of Kingdom people. Indeed, there is no clearer sign of the godlike self than a tender heart of unconditional love: "Love is of God" (1 John 4:7b). Or as Merton expressed so beautifully to an Italian Cistercian, "Love is the epiphany of God in our poverty."[66]

For Thomas Merton, love of neighbor is virtually synonymous with the spiritual life. There is no dichotomy between love of God and love of neighbor, as the false self would have us believe. Writing of the fourth-century Christians who went into the desert to live radical lives of prayer and asceticism, Merton notes their insistence "on the primacy of love over everything else in the spiritual life: over knowledge, gnosis, asceticism, contemplation, solitude, prayer." He then summarizes:

> Love in fact is the spiritual life, and without it all the other exercises of the spirit, however lofty, are emptied of content and become mere illusions. The more lofty they are, the more dangerous the illusion.[67]

Merton once described authentic love like this:

> Love is not itself
> Until it knows it is frail
> And can go wrong
>
> ...
>
> Love can never really begin
> Until both lovers
> Are bankrupt
>
> Love runs best
> When it seems to break down
> When no amount of driving

[66] Ibid., letter to Dom Francis Decroix, dated August 21, 1967, p. 157.
[67] Thomas Merton, *The Wisdom of the Desert: Sayings From the Desert Fathers of the Fourth Century* (New York: New Directions, 1961), p. 17.

Can rev it
No amount of gas
Can make it go
Love runs well
When it runs by itself
Without the help of man....[68]

No wonder love is the sign of the presence of
Dream-keepers. For in this godlike quality, a person imitates
Abba in the radical identification with the other. The lover
breaks away from the gravitational pull of the false self and
empties oneself into the world of the beloved. A lover
renounces the temptation to make the beloved an object of
self-gratification or a good business investment. A lover also
renounces the need to be in control, to be "in the driver's
seat."

Love runs best when it runs out of gas, "when it runs by
itself without the help of man." Such an act of "bankruptcy"
can only be done by the grace of God. Thus "love is of God."

But loving others can also open up the proverbial "can of
worms," the struggle with sexuality. And both celibates and
the married know the struggle. Fidelity to celibacy and
fidelity to marriage vows—each has its own unique trials and
temptations. But both celibate and married are called to let
"Thy Kingdom come" in the sexual dimension of life as in all
others.

The biggest temptation for many vowed religious is to
renounce their sexuality and become "asexual for Jesus." But
as Merton put it:

The capacity for human sexual love is not just a department
of one's life which you can lock out on entering the
monastery and forget about.... A person *has* to *really* face
this business of this instinct in our life and *really* negotiate

---

[68] Thomas Merton, "Six Love Letters," letter "v," in *Eighteen Poems* (New York:
New Directions, 1985).

it in our life.[69]

When celibate religious fear their sexuality, repress it, or escape from relationships in order to preserve their vow, they become prisoners of the false self. Repressed appetites go underground and find release in unconscious or unhealthy ways. All our basic appetites must be "faced and negotiated," as Merton stated. To "face" sexual desires means to accept them as part of our humanity and respect them as a precious gift from God. The drive for union which is the ultimate aim of the sexual appetite can be "negotiated" and sublimated through deep, loving friendships with others and a daily, consistent prayer life. Sexual energy can be released in a healthy way through exercise and recreation. Celibates who ignore their sexuality risk living petty, sterile and lonely lives.

But celibacy should not be reduced merely to "facing and negotiating" the sexual appetite. It is more importantly one expression of the Kingdom's unconditional love, especially for the poor, needy and forgotten. Celibates are challenged to stretch their hearts from east to west, like the hands of Jesus on the cross. They are challenged to be open and available to all people in a most unique way. Without love, celibacy becomes slavery to the false self. "[I]f I hand over my body so that I may boast, but do not have love, I gain nothing" (1 Corinthians 13:3).

For married keepers of God's Dream, Merton urges the tearing down of any mental walls that would separate Divine love from sexual love. He says that sexual intercourse is pure when it gives a rightful place to "all that is material, sensuous, fleshly, emotional, passionate, etc." between the

[69] Thomas Merton, "Love and the Search for God" (Kansas City, Mo.: Credence Cassettes), tape AA 2078.

married partners. Its aim is fundamentally love's freedom of expression: "to liberate in [the lovers] all the capacity for love and for the expression of love that would be truly and fully authentic in their peculiar circumstances."[70]

Merton is not suggesting "if it feels good, do it." He is aware that motivations can sometimes be mixed and self-centered. But like all love, sexual love is pure when the lover dies to the demands of the false self for the sake of the beloved and the situation in which the lovers find themselves.

Married Dream-keepers experience their marital love as a celebration of God's love and a prayer of praise. The sexual expression of their love is not reduced to slavish obedience to norms of morality. Rather, it attends to and incorporates the particular needs of each partner and the unique history shared between them. More importantly, this expression of love is never dissociated from the larger reality of love which challenges each spouse to die to the false self. God is given glory and the Kingdom comes every time a married couple gives free, creative and joyful sexual expression to the unique selfless love that God has incarnated in their lives through the gift of one another.

Surrender to the Present

Truth is sometimes stranger than fiction. As I write this chapter, the friary has received word of the death of Father Larry. Father Larry was literally in the midst of being transferred from our retirement home to a nursing home where he could receive the additional medical attention he needed. He resisted the transfer. He told one of the friars this

[70] Thomas Merton, "Purity," in *Love and Living* (New York: Bantam Books, 1980), pp. 103-105.

morning, "The only way they are going to move me is over my dead body!" He fought the nurses as they tried to help him into the back seat of the automobile. When the guardian of the community got into the driver's seat and turned the ignition key, he looked in his rear view mirror and Father Larry was slumped over in the back seat, the victim of a heart attack. Through the final moments of his life, he was still fighting to stay in control.

The false self refuses to let go. It insists on having *its* will be done, whatever that may be. It refuses to stand before the present with open, receptive hands.

The root of so much stress and so much emotional suffering is refusing to accept what is out of my control: namely, what life is presenting me at this very moment. The Gospel of Luke presents a rare glimpse of Jesus going through precisely this kind of emotional suffering.

Jesus' agony in the garden was so tremendous "his sweat became like great drops of blood falling down on the ground" (Luke 22:44). In his final hours, Jesus was under great stress as he confronted what he apparently thought was the end of his ministry and life. He did not want to totally accept and surrender to the present moment before him. The false self was fighting for control of the situation. "Father, if you are willing, take this cup away from me." But the true self saw the betrayer's hand and added, "[N]ot my will but yours be done" (Luke 22:42).

Like Jesus, Dream-keepers and Kingdom people live in the present moment, accepting what it brings them, surrendering to the unexpected and unknown. They surrender to the mysterious ways of God even when they do not understand. "[M]y thoughts are not your thoughts, nor are your ways my ways, says the LORD" (Isaiah 55:8). They renounce the false self's compulsion to dominate and control every moment, to pray "Not your will, Lord, but *mine* be done!" They trust in the reality of Divine love as the ground of their lives.

Fostering this Kingdom characteristic is just like learning how to float in water—and just as tricky. The more I actively try to float, the more I sink. My need to be in charge of the floating is my greatest obstacle. Floating requires trusting and surrendering. I give myself over to the water. Those rooted in the true self approach life in the same way. They bow before the mystery of life and say with Mary, "[L]et it be with me according to your word" (Luke 1:38).

This kind of surrender is the active side of patient endurance, a virtue on which traditional Chinese culture places a high moral value. The Chinese character for "endurance" or "patience" vividly portrays the pain, agony and challenge this Kingdom characteristic sometimes entails: "a knife in the heart."

Let me be very clear on this point. Surrender is not mere resignation or passivity to the problems of everyday life. I still take charge of my responsibilities. I must stand and fight against injustice and the continuation of evil in all its personal and social forms. I must actively promote peace and love by my actions. Yet some things in life, like physical illnesses and deaths of loved ones—"knives in the heart"— cannot be changed. They can only be endured. So I renounce the need to be in control, and I surrender with a confident faith and active trust in Abba. That means developing a spirituality which, when all is said and done, is confident to pray, "Lord, have it your way! Thy Kingdom come!" Kingdom people experience the present reality as God's Dream because they actively respond to the moment before them with open, receptive hands and a trust-filled heart.

Throughout Francis' life he practiced the art of letting go

of control and surrendering to the present. It appears to have become second nature to him by the time of his death.

While Francis was in the throes of his conversion, he renounced the false self's dreams of knighthood and worldly glory. The culminating moment of his conversion as he stood naked before the bishop and people of Assisi, was also a moment of letting go: of his inheritance, his family name, his father. As the Franciscan Order spread geographically and more men desired to join, the earlier expression of the Franciscan life had to give way to a more updated expression that incorporated thousands of friars. And so Francis had to let the pristine dream which motivated so much of his early religious life be reinterpreted for a new situation. At one point, he had to let go of the Order's leadership. And towards the end of his life, he had to renounce the luxury of good health.

The Italians have an expression, "As you live, so you die." It comes as no surprise then, when death came knocking on the door, Francis' spontaneous response was, "Welcome, Sister Death!" For Francis, death was simply another moment of doing what he had been doing all his life: renouncing control over the present moment; surrendering to the unexpected and the unknown.

Peace and Joy

The amazing thing about keepers of God's Dream is that they are unflappable! In the midst of the most intense and destructive storms, they still manage to maintain inner peace and calm. Saint Bonaventure considers this tranquillity to be the sixth and highest stage of one's progress in the love of God. He describes the person "as if in Noah's Ark where tempests cannot reach."[71]

Father Medard has grown old graciously. Ironically, some forty of those seventy-six years have been a living hell for him, both physically and psychologically. A bout with tuberculosis, an operation removing half his lung and fifteen other operations, including one on his heart, have left him with a frail physical presence. Surprisingly, though, he has more ministerial energy than most of the other friars with whom he lives.

Med has never been elected to any position among the friars. Frankly, one could say he was ostracized by his own religious community. Why? During the years of change after Vatican II Med was the rector of the Franciscan theology school. The older priests in the province and the faculty of the theology school thought that Med was too progressive. And the students? They thought he was just too conservative. Stuck in the middle and totally misunderstood, he had no friends or confidants among his own community.

Such physical trials coupled with his community's lack of appreciation and understanding would have turned many people bitter, angry, resentful. But not Med. Med has no guile, no axes to grind. Now, as he runs to have a second daily Mass for some forgotten nursing home patients or to walk his daily mile on the treadmill, he has a deep, abiding peace and joy.

I once asked Med how he survived the physical pains and emotional downs of his life. "Albert," he said, "there came a point in my life when I discovered that, no matter how terrible the storm raging around me may be, by the grace of God, I'm still in the boat and my Father is at the helm!"

Kingdom people like Father Medard are not naive,

[71] *The Triple Way* 2:11, *The Works of Bonaventure*, volume 1, "Mystical Opuscula" (Paterson, N.J.: St. Anthony Guild Press, 1960), p. 78.

irresponsible or living on another planet. They still experience disappointment, sadness and sorrow. However, they are not consumed or destroyed by these feelings. They know, as Julian of Norwich wrote, "in the end, all will be well and every manner of thing will be well."

Kingdom people live with the awareness that God is in the driver's seat: "My Father is at the helm!" or, as the old song says, "He's got the whole world in His hands." So Dream-keepers come back to the reality of the present moment and swim in the sun that shines upon them even during the worst of storms.

Moments of Mystery

The most difficult time for any Christian to keep the Dream of God alive and bear witness to the Kingdom is during a time of profound doubt, confusion, questioning and anxiety.

During such moments of mystery common sense fails; logic and good reasoning fall short. A person is challenged to a faith-walk in the darkness.

That illusive and forgotten member of the Holy Family, Joseph, is a good patron saint for such times. Job is another.

Imagine the confusion Joseph must have felt. His fiancée is pregnant and he is not the father of the child. An angel appears to him and tells him that Mary is pregnant by the Holy Spirit. Joseph is asked to take her into his home, to care for her and the child, and to name the child Jesus (Matthew 1:18-24).

We can almost sense Joseph's doubt and confusion, as well as the skepticism causing him to seriously consider divorcing Mary. "My fiancée is with child! Now someone says it is by the Holy Spirit! Common sense tells me that something is seriously wrong here." A moment of mystery. A call to walk in the darkness.

Then there is Job. This upright, God-fearing man suddenly confronts that age-old, mysterious question: Why do bad things happen to good people? Everything is taken away from this holy man: family, farm, health (Job 1:6-22). It makes no sense in the false self's understanding of life, justice and God. Job is challenged to live with a question, to live in a moment of mystery.

The stories of Job and Joseph are our stories. We have all been challenged to face mysterious questions, to live moments of mystery.

Philip and Ann take their faith seriously, are involved in their parish, and bring their Christian values to their work. They awaited the birth of their third child with joyful anticipation. But little Julie was born badly deformed. Now, just like Job, they are forced to live with mystery. There is no logic to it. It makes no sense.

Many people thought that Sally was being naive. But when her husband, after his two years of infidelity, begged to start their marriage all over again, Sally said yes. Hesitant and confused, like Joseph, she was taking a step into the darkness.

The phone call from the adoption agency proved to be a test of Sue and Andy's generosity and faith. The little boy, David, had been found in a plastic bag in a garbage dumpster. He was a few months old and severely brain-damaged. "We know you and Andy have been interested in a child. This one will be virtually impossible to place. You are our only hope. Will you accept him?"

Andy just could not walk away from such a child. Though he could easily understand Sue's initial opposition, his heart was not at peace. His mind and heart wrestled for a week. Convincing Sue, he returned the adoption agency's call. "Yes, we'll give little David a home." Like Joseph, Sue and Andy said yes to a moment of mystery that raised more questions than answers.

A friend of mine in his early forties announced to his wife one day: "I need some space. I need some time to be alone. I need some freedom." That precipitated a moment of mystery for my friend's wife of fifteen years. Like Job, she has to live with that confusing, heart-breaking question: "Why do bad things happen to good people?"

We have all known that question which haunted Job in his misery. Like Joseph, we have all experienced moments when we felt called to do something that we really did not understand with our heads but still felt in our hearts we had to do. We all know what it is like to feel as if someone is calling us, but we have no idea where we are going or who is the one calling. We have to find the courage to befriend such moments of mystery.

When confronted with a moment of mystery, the false self immediately attempts to make sense of it and understand it: "It's God's will" or "This will make me a better person" or "No pain, no gain. No guts, no glory." It tries to put mystery into a logical category of understanding and comprehension. With ax in hand, it picks away at mystery, hoping to crack it open. It analyzes mystery like a specimen under a microscope.

The agony of the mid-life crisis has no rational explanation. The birth of a sick child defies all logic. The need to follow one's heart can never be rationally explained. As Pascal said, "The heart has its reasons which reason knows nothing of."

To try to force a moment of mystery into a logical framework is to violate it. Mystery is mystery. The more the false self tries to understand it, the more unintelligible mystery becomes.

Joseph would have been beating his head against a brick wall if he had tried to make sense of the Annunciation. And those "logical" people who criticized him for taking a pregnant woman into his home and marrying her, betray their own ignorance of the ways of God. "[M]y thoughts are not your thoughts, nor are your ways my ways" (Isaiah 55:8).

There is an ancient Islamic story about a man searching under a street lamp for a key he has dropped.

A neighbor sees him searching and says, "What are you looking for?"

"My key," the man replies. "I've dropped it."

The neighbor joins the midnight search for the key under the street lamp, but he does not find it either.

"Where did you drop it?" his neighbor asks.

The man said, "Down the road there about fifty yards."

The neighbor, somewhat puzzled, asks, "Well, why are you looking here?"

And the man said, "Because there is more light here."

Dream-keepers are often forced to leave the illuminated pigpen of pat answers and go on a sometimes-painful pilgrimage into the darkness of faith. They take the plunge of mature faith with all of its doubts and uncertainties.

Walking with mystery is the deepest and most agonizing form of poverty, for it means renouncing the "riches of the mind" and returning to the heart. To quote the wisdom of the fox found in the book *The Little Prince*: "It is only with the heart that one sees rightly; what is essential is invisible to the eye."

A man went to the guard at the Gate of the Future and said: "Sir, give me a light that I may tread safely into the unknown!"

And the wise old guard at the Gate of the Future replied: "My friend, go out into the darkness. Follow thy heart and put thine hand into the Hand of God. That shall be to thee better than light and safer than a known way."

We all know the utter sadness which overcomes us when we strike an alliance with the false self and attempt to control, imprison or suppress mystery as if it were a rebellious child or a criminal. We know the endless restlessness which consumes us when we sweep those mysterious longings of our hearts under the carpet, refusing to acknowledge their presence. We know the deep-seated frustration that is a result of our disrespectful treatment of those irrational wishes as wild animals that need to be caged and, most often, tamed.

A moment of mystery, from a sick child to the departure of a spouse, from the acceptance of my sexuality to a gut-level feeling that demands fidelity, is not a rebellious criminal that must be imprisoned. It is not a wild animal that must be subdued or tamed.

A true moment of mystery is the bud of a flower. A Dream-keeper allows it to unfold in its own way and in its own time. A person rooted in the true self nurtures the mystery and waits for it to blossom. "The meanings we are capable of discovering are never sufficient. The true meaning has to be revealed. It has to be 'given.'"[72]

That only happens, of course, by walking with the mystery. "My friend, go out into the darkness. Follow thy heart and put thine hand into the Hand of God. That shall be to thee better than light and safer than a known way."

While on a preaching mission in Cameroon, West Africa, I met a blind man by the name of John. I asked him in the

---

[72] Merton, *The New Man*, p. 13.

course of our conversation if he found it difficult not having eyesight. He surprised me with his response. "Don't you know? Haven't you experienced it? After all, when it comes to living our faith, we all walk as blind people."

The essence of faith is blindness. "[E]ven though you do not see him now, you believe in him" (1 Peter 1:8). It is a way of living, not seeing. We renounce the false self's desire to understand and rationalize which offers so much security and, like Peter, we take that agonizing and precarious step onto water (Matthew 14:22-33). What is important is not how far we get; the important thing is that we take the step. Spiritual progress is measured "in" the stepping, not in the size of the gait. As Father Medard once told me, "Get out of the boat. Step onto the water. And the secret is, don't look at your feet!"

As we walk in darkness with the mystery, as we journey with the doubts of mid-life down a path we have never been before, as we stand before the mystery of a sick child or the loss of a beloved person, gradually the mystery begins to reveal its delicate, fragile blossom. Like a late-blooming flower, the mystery begins to disclose its own unique secrets and answers, secrets and answers we never may have dreamt of when first confronted with the moment of mystery. How many times have we heard ourselves say, "I would have never thought that something this good could have come out of something that started so badly" or "If you would have told me back then what I know now, I would not have been so frightened."

German poet Rainer Maria Rilke once gave this advice to a young poet:

> Be patient toward all that is unsolved in your heart. Try to love the questions themselves. Do not seek the answers which cannot be given because you would not be able to live

them. And the point is, to live everything. *Live* the questions now. Perhaps you will then gradually, without noticing it, live along some distant day into the answers.[73]

Being at home with self, others and God makes a Dream-keeper strong and patient enough to live with a question. Constantly in labor, the true self waits for something deep within to be born. Quietly the mystery blossoms for those who surrender in faith. An answer, sometimes as mysterious as the question, is given. For Joseph, the mystery of the Annunciation blossomed into the miracle of Christmas. For those in mid-life transition, the devastating questions which challenge and threaten everything the false self spent the first half of life working for and earning, gradually become silent. They then begin the wonderful journey that is the usual task of the second half of life: the interior journey, the journey back home. The lonely and frightening walk to embrace one's own sexuality brings a person one step closer to self-acceptance and personal integration. Even the profound mystery of a deformed child flowers into the beauty, challenge and gift of raising another sacrament of the Divine.

Thomas Merton offers a beautiful prayer to pray before a moment of mystery. It is the prayer, no doubt, that Joseph prayed the morning after his famous dream. It is the prayer of Dream-keepers and Kingdom people when they are called to mature faith. When we are called to befriend mystery, to live with a question, to grope in the darkness, this prayer is a good way to pray "Thy Kingdom come":

> My Lord God, I have no idea where I am going. I do not see the road ahead of me. I cannot know for certain where it will end. Nor do I really know myself, and the fact that I think I

---

[73] Rainer Maria Rilke, *Letters to a Young Poet*, translated by M.D. Herter Norton (New York: W.W. Norton and Company, 1954), p. 35.

am following your will does not mean that I am actually doing so. But I believe that the desire to please you does in fact please you. And I hope I have that desire in all that I am doing. I hope that I will never do anything apart from that desire. And I know that if I do this you will lead me by the right road, though I may know nothing about it. Therefore I will trust you always though I may seem to be lost and in the shadow of death. I will not fear, for you are ever with me, and you will never leave me to face my perils alone.[74]

Points for Reflection

How do I keep God's Dream of peace, love and justice alive in my own life? Is my life oriented towards the Kingdom of God?

When did I first experience God's love "not as an abstraction" but as *the* reality of life?

Do I sincerely try to open my heart in love to others? Who are the most difficult to love?

How well do I accept the present moment and surrender to it with a trust-filled heart? Am I often frustrated by my fighting against life? Can I pray with Mary, "Let this moment be done to me as you say"?

Does the knowledge of God's presence in my life bring peace and joy—even in the midst of storms?

What have been the moments of mystery in my life?

[74] Merton, *Thoughts in Solitude*, p. 83.

How did I initially respond to them? How did the mystery unfold?

CHAPTER SIX

'Thy Will Be Done on Earth as It Is in Heaven'

P raying for the Kingdom of God implies that we are committed to doing the will of God. But when people talk about God's will, they sometimes give the impression that all they need do is "figure it out." They seem to think "God's will" has been predetermined for them since the moment of their conception. Thomas Merton called such an approach to the will of God "pagan." He went on to add, this "is the idea not of God's will but of fate."[75]

Discerning God's will is not the same thing as "picking God's brain" to determine one's fate in life. Our free will is one of the most precious gifts God has given to us. And God chooses never to violate it. God desires human free will to collaborate, not collapse, before the great Dream of the Kingdom. We are coadjutors, not computers.

So despite what some people might be tempted to think, a healthy process of discernment does not end in the personal renunciation of free will in order "to do what God wants." Thomas Merton says:

> Too often a legalistic concept of the will of God leads to a hypocritical falsification of the interior life. Do we not often

[75] Thomas Merton, "Renunciation and Contemplation" (Kansas City, Mo.: Credence Cassettes),tape AA 2073.

unconsciously take it for granted that God is a harsh lawgiver, without interest in the thoughts and desires of our own hearts, seeking only to impose upon us the arbitrary dictates of His own inscrutable, predetermined plans? And yet, as St. Paul has said, we are called to *collaborate* with God....[76]

One of the paradoxes in the spiritual life is that a person must be truly free in order to be a servant of the Kingdom. A contemporary understanding of discernment, therefore, must move beyond the pagan notion of "figuring out my fate" and then passively submitting to the "will of God." It must free a person to participate dynamically and creatively in helping to build the Kingdom of God. It must help us bring our personal freedom into communion with the freedom of God. This is the deepest meaning of doing the will of God.

The Head and the Heart

The process of discernment does not abandon intelligence, good judgment or common sense. Yet it is not simply an intellectual affair. Discernment also gives attention to the desires, affections and yearnings of the heart. It is precisely through these, John of the Cross reminds us in the Commentary to the *Spiritual Canticle*, that God communicates to the soul. To ignore what we want or desire in a particular situation not only violates personal integrity but refuses to listen to God's effort to communicate with us.

So often those seeking help in discernment will describe their attraction to a particular decision, saying, "Father, that's what I want, but I don't know what God wants!" They assume God's will to be something different from their own.

---

[76] Merton, *Spiritual Direction and Meditation*, p. 27.

Of course, discernment of the will of God cannot be reduced simply to our whims and wants. That's why every act of discernment demands walking the delicate balance between head and heart. Indeed, five-sixths of discernment is making a wise, prudent head-heart decision.

Head-Heart Decisionmaking

Five factors need to be taken into consideration if we are to maintain the delicate balance between head and heart: my past history; my potential; my present identity; my hopes, dreams and desires; my free heart.

My past history. My upbringing, the values which I was taught and which I assimilated, the deficiencies of my family life and their psychological effects upon me, and my education—these all have played a role in bringing me to this present moment of decisionmaking. Added to that are my responses to past situations and the consequences which resulted. The elements of my past have a limiting, though not necessarily crippling, effect upon the present.

If I only have had a grammar school education, for example, I have to take an honest look at my desire to become a lawyer or a college professor. The lack of higher education does not mean I am incapable of going back to school or that I lack the intellectual abilities to fulfill my dream. It simply means I need to be prudent and realistic about the role of education in my life. My past can narrow my possibilities or options.

My potential. My past tends to limit me, but my talents and abilities open up possibilities. These God-given personal gifts make me a "diamond in the rough." Talents and abilities are the keys that help to unlock the future. They can allow an adult who only had a grammar school education to become a lawyer or a college professor. In any important moment of decision, there is always a tension between my past and my potential. The past "stacks the deck" against me, but my talents and abilities are "wild cards" in the game of life.

My present identity. My past and my potential come together in my present identity with its commitments and responsibilities. My present commitment to others—in marriage, in the single life, or in a vowed community life—as well as the responsibilities which such commitments place upon me need to be respected. This requires dialogue with the significant people in my present situation. I cannot simply step away from the present to walk into the future. The future flows out of the present; it does not ignore it.

My hopes, dreams and desires. These are the most elusive part of making any good decision. Sometimes unconscious, my hopes and dreams are the gasoline of life. They give me ambition, energy and meaning. They fuel my vitality and passion. They bridge the chasm which my doubts and fears dig between present and future. They give me the courage to take a risk, to step out in faith in spite of the protestations of the false self.

Thomas Merton used to ask his novices two important questions: "What do you want out of life?" and "What's stopping you from getting it?" These questions can also help all of us get in touch with our motivating dreams and desires—as well as with the fears, doubts and obstacles which often frustrate them.

The power and importance of dreams and desires should never be underestimated. Merton insists that some desires "represent a possibility of *a special, spontaneous and personal gift which [the penitent] alone can make to God. If there is some gift which he alone can give, then almost certainly God* asks that gift from him, and a holy, humble, and sincere desire may be one of the signs that God asks it!"[77]

Hopes, dreams and desires are explicit manifestations of the unconscious. Paying attention to them is therefore essential to the discernment process.

My free heart. What option or decision makes me peaceful and happy? Which one do I find most appealing and attractive? Feelings can confirm so much in the spiritual life as long as the heart is *free.*

But that, of course, is the catch: The heart must be free. If I am still content to be among the pigs, promoting the false self, then I must hold the response of my heart in suspicion. For example, a strongly felt surge of initial resistance to one particular option may be an indicator not that this would be an unwise decision, but, more fundamentally, that some aspect of the false self is being threatened or attacked.

I need to be as internally free from the false self's agenda as I can consciously be before I can give the response of my heart its rightful place in the decisionmaking process. Only after he freed himself from the false self's agenda to be a famous knight could Francis of Assisi truly follow his heart in serving the Master.[78]

Pete had been a religious for six years. He was not really happy. But he was not unhappy either. He just assumed that his emotionless approach to life was part of his introverted personality.

Pete was making a thirty-day retreat in preparation for his final profession of vows when what started out as an innocent question by his retreat director provoked a startling revelation in Pete's life. The question: What do *you* really want?

[77] Ibid., pp. 27-28.
[78] Celano's *Second Life* 6, *Omnibus of Sources*, p. 365.

Pete felt truly secure and confident about his ministerial plans to work with Hispanics. They capitalized on his ability to learn another language and be comfortable in another culture. But being a "religious" was another matter. Something "clicked" inside of Pete as soon as he allowed himself to be objective enough to reflect upon his motivations for being a religious: His religious vocation was more a product of parental pressure than of personal desire. During the next five days, Pete's heart became restless as he realized more and more that, committed to the Church though he was, religious life was not where he belonged.

Once he crossed that bridge and gave himself permission to ask himself what *he* wanted, Pete came alive emotionally for the first time that he could remember. His heart was set free and he started feeling emotions: relief, happiness, inner peace.

His heart, once freed from the desire to please his parents, ultimately held the key for the best decision he could make about his future. Today Pete is happily married and working for the Spanish-speaking apostolate in a diocese in the eastern part of the country.

The five above-mentioned factors converge at the time of decisionmaking and form the jury. The first three deal with the head and the last two deal with the heart. As they begin to talk to one another, a decision begins to emerge and I find myself leaning in the direction of a wise, prudent head-heart decision. That decision is sometimes confirmed when the head and heart connect in *felt knowledge*: Something "clicks" inside and I know what I must do. But even without the "click," the decision is there for my true self to claim and act on.

The Faith Factor

A wise, prudent head-heart decision is not the end point of the process for discerning the will of God. We must also consider the faith factor, or the baptismal response to the situation.

When Adam and Eve forgot God's Dream for creation, their original sin was like a stone dropping in a calm pond. The ripples from that stone have echoed through history. The false self appeared and creation was thrown off balance.

As a descendant of Adam and Eve, I am affected by the ripples of original sin. I am also constantly tempted to "do my own thing" and ignore Jesus' strong example of what it means to keep the Dream and build God's Kingdom. My baptismal incorporation into the life and death of Jesus, however, is a public commitment to keep the Dream alive; to help creation stay on track; to build God's Kingdom of peace, justice and love; to come home to what I already have and who I really am, my godlike and true self.

A wise, prudent head-heart decision becomes a discernment of the will of God when the decisionmaking process seriously incorporates questions like these: How can I uniquely contribute to God's Kingdom in this situation? How can I best make God's Dream a reality here and now? How can I foster the Kingdom's peace, justice and love? Which option best helps to manifest these characteristics?

God's will is not some predetermined, preordained decision from on high which I must struggle to figure out and then buckle under to obey. As Merton told the young monks of Gethsemani:

> Your vocation isn't something that's in a filing cabinet in heaven that is kept secret from you and then sort of whipped out at the Last Judgment and [God says], "You missed, buddy! You didn't guess right." But your vocation, or

anything in life, is an invitation on the part of God which you're not supposed to guess and you're not supposed to figure out. It's something you work out by free response.[79]

We are left to freely shape the gift of life that God has given us in light of the original Dream for all creation. Through our upbringing, talents, abilities and gifts, God presents each one of us with canvas, paint and brushes. We become the artists of our lives. Discerning God's will is nothing more than responding with my unique, gifted contribution to God's Dream for creation. And so the portrait of my life becomes my gift back to God.

When I make the major decisions of my life in light of my unique contribution to the Kingdom of God, I become a Dream-keeper, too. This is what it means to "imitate Christ"—to do my part in building the Kingdom and sharing God's Dream with all whom I encounter.

"But that sounds mighty vague and general! I could easily make a mistake with the best of intentions." Yes, that's true. And that fear can lead to some false notions about "imitating Christ." Brother John the Simple mimicked Saint Francis in every act of spitting, coughing, weeping, praying and the like,[80] but that kind of naive imitation becomes a subtle form of slavery. It could even be an expression of the false self's pride. The real guard against mistakes in discerning God's will is *community*.

Authentic discernment is never a private, individual process. Though it demands honest self-knowledge, it is always done in a communal setting: with family and friends, those affected by one's decision, and one's spiritual director *in dialogue with* the Scriptures and Church, both institutional and prophetic. One should beware of any

[79] Merton, "Renunciation and Contemplation."
[80] Celano's *Second Life* 190, *Omnibus of Sources*, p. 514.

discernment process made privately or that needs to be kept secret. Refusal to dialogue and fear of community are indications that the false self is speaking.

Catching the Dream

I arrived for my first visit to the Grand Canyon rather late in the evening. It was already dark. But my curiosity and excitement at seeing the Grand Canyon would not keep until morning. So I went to the southern rim to take a look. And all I saw through the darkness was a big hole. No splendor, no majesty. I couldn't help but think that this was another one of America's great tourist traps. I went back to my tent, decided that my disappointment was not going to ruin this vacation, and fell asleep.

The following morning I got up before dawn. For years I had heard about the miracle of sunrise over the Grand Canyon. So I started back to the rim, careful not to let my excitement or anticipation get the better of me. As the morning sun inched its way into the sky and offered light to the earth, the "big hole" suddenly started coming alive with shades of red, purple, blue and yellow. With hundreds of other people, I found myself "ooh-ing" and "aah-ing" over God's daily miracle in northern Arizona. It was the same old canyon as the night before but, in the light of the morning sun, everything looked so different.

Likewise, the more I consciously allow the light of Christ received at Baptism to shine in my life and challenge me, the more clearly I will see the part that I can play in the Kingdom of God. It will be the same old me but, seen in the light of my commitment to God's Dream, it will seem so different. My actions and attitudes will take on a deeper meaning. Some of my commitments and obligations might have to change, not because of infidelity, but precisely because of the deepening appreciation for my Baptism and my maturing responsibility and free response to the Dream of the Kingdom. It's not a question of "what God wants of me." It's a question of "what I want to give to God."

Kathy is an exceptionally bright, articulate lawyer. After graduating from the University of Chicago, she started working for a large and prestigious law firm. Within five years she had climbed the ladder of success. During those years, however, she also began to see and experience the harsh injustices of the American legal system. "Basically, Father, only the rich can afford to have justice served," she told me at our first spiritual direction session.

After much prayer and a weekend retreat, Kathy decided that she risked losing her faith in God and the system of law if she did not make a change. So she went into private practice and quietly began accepting more and more pro bono cases. "They don't help feed my husband and daughter," she said, "but they keep me in touch with my Christian values."

But that wasn't the end of Kathy's discernment process. Successful as Kathy has been in private practice, Kathy continues to allow the light of Christ to challenge her in ways that never cease to amaze me. She has now temporarily given up the law practice and begun graduate studies in Christian ethics. Her dream is to teach future lawyers how to bring together the practice of law with the teachings of the gospel.

The movie *Tucker* was based upon a true story about a man who had a dream to build a new kind of automobile in the suburbs of Chicago. It died a rather quick death as a movie, but it is memorable in one respect. At one point one of the characters turned to a friend of this automobile visionary and said, "Don't get close to him! You may catch his dream."

Catching the Dream—that's the whole point of the spiritual life: The more I catch the Dream, the closer I get to home and to the godlike self. And in catching the Dream, my will comes into communion with the will of God.

This communion is not slavery. Catching the Dream triggers a deep transformation that frees a person's whole being—the mind, heart, feelings, emotions, desires—from bondage to the false self. This interior transformation becomes evident in one's actions. One adopts a life-style that increasingly gives witness to the Kingdom characteristics of peace, justice and love. That interior transformation is the greatest glory of humanity and the truest meaning of the imitation of Christ. As Merton told the novices of Gethsemani:

> A saint is a person who when he does his own will, is doing the will of God.... The root of his willing is in God.... The greatest glory of a creature is to act freely as the instrument of God.... His acts are Christ's.[81]

The Letter to Brother Leo

The Letter to Brother Leo is one of two handwritten parchments of Francis still preserved today. Though relatively short, it is a precious document of primitive Franciscan spirituality. Though we do not know the exact circumstances surrounding its composition, we can infer that it is a summary of the saint's conversation with Brother Leo, his confessor and close companion, about the nature of discernment:

[81] Thomas Merton, "The Vow of Conversion" (Kansas City, Mo.: Credence Cassettes), tape AA 2228.

Brother Leo, [wish] your Brother Francis health and peace!

I speak to you, my son, as a mother. I place all the words which we spoke on the road in this phrase, briefly and [as] advice. And afterwards, if it is necessary for you to come to me for counsel, I say this to you: In whatever way it seems best to you to please the Lord God and to follow His footprints and His poverty, do this with the blessing of God and my obedience. And if you believe it necessary for the well-being of your soul, or to find comfort, and you wish to come to me, Leo, come![82]

Francis places the responsibility of "pleasing the Lord God" upon Brother Leo's own personal initiative. ("Pleasing the Lord" is often associated in the saint's writings with the will of God.) This suggests that the saint's companion must have been a man of extraordinary self-knowledge and brutal self-honesty, a man free of the compulsions and addictions of the false self. Leo was a man committed to the Dream. He was a man whose judgments, Francis knew, could be trusted.

But even the spiritually mature are in need of the counsel of others. Discernment is never a private affair. So Francis makes himself available to offer advice just in case Brother Leo finds it necessary.

This letter offers a Franciscan approach to discernment for those who have truly caught the Dream of the Kingdom. From the Franciscan perspective, true obedience to the will of God, in imitation of Christ, is a positive expression of a person's freedom and creativity. "To please God" is simply to discover one's own unique way of contributing to Jesus' Kingdom of peace, justice and love. It is what we pray for when we say, "Thy will be done on earth as it is in heaven."

---

[82] *Francis and Clare: The Complete Works*, trans. by Regis J. Armstrong, O.F.M. Cap., and Ignatius C. Brady, O.F.M. (Mahwah, N.J.: Paulist Press, 1982), pp. 47-48.

Points for Reflection

What is the first thing I think of when I hear the words "the will of God for me"?

What was the most recent head-heart decision that I made? Did I give any consideration to my baptismal commitment during its discernment process?

How open am I to dialogue and discussion in my personal method of discernment? Do I simply inform people of my decisions or do I allow myself to be "informed"?

Have I "caught the Dream" of the Kingdom?

CHAPTER SEVEN

'Give Us This Day Our Daily Bread'

Before God, my dependency and need are exposed like open sores. I can stand only as a beggar with hands outstretched. To pray "Give us this day our daily bread" is to recognize my absolute and existential poverty before God.

Everything is a gift. I can claim nothing as my own. I proclaim everything as a grace: my looks, my personality, my friends, my talents, my very existence. Abba, the Divine Almsgiver, transforms my poverty and dependency into the experience of life in abundance.

That was the spiritual insight which gave birth to the voluntary poverty of Francis of Assisi. Francis' poverty was not simply an expression of self-denial and mortification—as had been the case in the monastic tradition. Francis' poverty was a radical affirmation that God alone is the source of everything that is good. God is the one who clothes us, feeds us, provides for our every need. Voluntary poverty gives living witness to the Divine Almsgiver.

Francis compares those taking personal credit for the grace of God in their life to Adam's eating the apple: "A man eats of the tree that brings knowledge of good when he claims that his good will comes from himself alone and prides himself on the good that God says and does in him."[83]

---

[83] Admonition 2, *Omnibus of Sources*, p. 79.

To pray, "Give us this day our daily bread," is to recognize the grace, goodness and generosity of God working in and through our lives.

Many people only come to an awareness of God as a faithful and trustworthy Almsgiver through personal tragedy. Suffering can reveal the false self's illusion of independent self-sufficiency. It can challenge one to return to the authentic self: a poor beggar whose very existence is dependent upon Abba.

After my father's suicide and burial, we discovered that he had a large debt. We were forced to sell the family home and automobile. My mother had been a homemaker up until that time. She now had to learn a skill and find employment to support three children still at home. There must have been many times when she prayed, "Give us this day our daily bread." And God did. Abba, the Divine Almsgiver, provided for us.

When the carpet is pulled from underneath our feet, we need not worry. When we are forced to admit our need and dependence, we need not be anxious. Dream-keepers surrender to the present moment and trust in the providence of God.

Jesus said: "Therefore I tell you, do not worry about your life, what you will eat or what you will drink, or about your body, what you will wear" (Matthew 6:25). For if Abba can feed the birds who do not sow or reap and clothe the wildflowers which do not work or spin, Abba will certainly provide much more for us.

Jesus reminded us that the Divine Almsgiver is invested in our needs. Abba is on our side:

> Ask, and it will be given you; search, and you will find; knock, and the door will be opened for you. For everyone who asks receives, and everyone who searches finds, and for

everyone who knocks, the door will be opened. Is there anyone among you who, if your child asks for bread, will give a stone? Or if the child asks for a fish, will give a snake? If you then, who are evil, know how to give good gifts to your children, how much more will your Father in heaven give good things to those who ask him! (Matthew 7:7-11)

When personal tragedies push us to the brink of despair, we remain the subjects of Divine attention. When we are stripped of possessions, friends, beliefs and even God-images, we are, nevertheless, the beloved. Abba is committed to us. Abba is eager to provide for us. Abba will meet all our needs.

'Become Like Children'

Just look at a child who is lost at the zoo or in the grocery store. The look of terror says it all. Children have no illusions. They know they are helpless and dependent. They know where their toys, food and love come from. Though they may be unable to verbalize it, children know they are totally dependent on Mom and Dad.

To pray the petition, "Give us this day our daily bread," is to be childlike and admit my dependency, helplessness and need. For as Jesus challenges us, "Truly I tell you, unless you change and become like children, you will never enter the kingdom of heaven" (Matthew 18:3).

While a deacon, I became friends with one of our elderly friars who was approaching his eightieth birthday. We loved to tease one another. Father Harold would jokingly mutter about the radical young friars and I would complain about the old guys. In the midst of our bantering, I once naively said, "Harold, I will never get old!" Father Harold, with a twinkle in his eye, solemnly responded, "Albert, that's because you will never grow up!"

Never to grow up—never to outgrow God. That is a goal of the spiritual life. Never to foolishly think that we can make it on our own without God or grace.

The false self tries to convince me that the really important things in life are based upon what *I* do, upon *my* abilities. If I buy into that illusion, I begin to take charge. I begin wielding power. I become manipulative. I insist upon things being done my way. I demand what I think is rightfully mine and, like the prodigal son, off I go!

This independent, self-sufficient approach to life is the fundamental sin of so many of us. It is the refusal of grace. It is the failure to acknowledge Abba as the Divine Almsgiver. It is Adam and Eve reaching for the apple all over again.

But, luckily, self-sufficiency can take us only so far. Sooner or later we run up against a brick wall. We get a sudden glimpse into our existential self-deficiency. We finish eating the apple and discover, a few hours later, that we are hungry again. We spend all our inheritance on fun and games only to worry about how we will buy tomorrow's bread. We gradually realize where we actually are and where we truly belong.

And then come the questions which attack the agenda of the false self. In the words of the prodigal son, "How many of my father's hired hands have bread enough and to spare, but here I am dying of hunger! I will get up and go to my father" (Luke 15:17-18a).

Preaching has always come easily to me. Even back in high school, my friends would tease, "Wherever two or three are gathered, there is Albert preaching." I spent the first ten years of my ordained ministry promoting my talent. After doctoral studies and a brief stint on a retreat house staff, I began preaching parish missions full time. Booked ahead for two years at a time, I crisscrossed the country—and several continents—three weeks of every month. In just over two years, I had earned 120,000 frequent-flyer points on United Airlines.

I enjoyed the life-style of the "Yuppie Priest," as my oldest brother called it. I met some wonderful people. I saw places I never dreamt I would see—from the tomb of Saint Francis to the Great Wall of China. (A great recruitment slogan: "Become a friar and see the world!") And, from the many letters that I have received, I know I touched lots of people along the way.

So why did I give up that "life-style of the poor and infamous"? Because I gradually came to realize that I was not preaching the gospel; I was preaching myself. I had convinced myself of the very lie that I so desperately tried to convince my listeners of: "You need to listen to me. My words can change your life." I began to feel like a fraud. And then one day it smacked me right in the face: All my self-promotion had gotten me was life in a pigpen—in business class at 37,000 feet!

That encounter with the illusions of the false self threw me into a tailspin and began a three-year process of discerning my unique contribution to God's Dream of the Kingdom. It rekindled a childhood dream that I had put on the back burner when the fame of a preacher became so attractive and enticing. I live in Taiwan now where I am reminded constantly of my self-deficiency as I struggle to learn a new language and live in a culture totally different from my own. Preaching is constantly asked of me, but now it is not a result of my self-promotion.

Giving up "my" preaching ministry was one of the toughest decisions I've ever made. It was also one of the most precious graces from God. The sin of my self-*sufficiency* was transformed into the painful awareness of my self-*deficiency*.

Life in the pigpen brings us to the awareness that we are far from home. "[W]here sin increased, grace abounded all the more" (Romans 5:20). And responding to the generous alms of God's grace is the secret to spiritual maturity.

The false self promotes the self-sufficient image of spiritual maturity. In reality, however, the spiritually mature are totally poor. Merton said:

> The whole Christian life is a life in which the further a person progresses, the more he has to depend directly on God and it's not the other way around at all.... The more we progress, the less we are self-sufficient. The more we progress, the poorer we get so that the man who has progressed most, is totally poor—he has to depend directly on God. He's got nothing left in himself.[84]

Growth in the spiritual life is measured by one's awareness of absolute dependence upon Abba and one's continual petition for daily bread. The true self is a living incarnation of the petition, "Give us this day our daily bread." A great paradox in the spiritual life, indeed: To mature is to become a child, poor, needy, helpless and dependent. "Unless you turn and become like children, you will not enter the kingdom of heaven." It's just another way of saying that heaven is not earned; it is given.

Merton once distinguished two kinds of spirituality. The first way, based in the Synoptic Gospels, is characterized by active faith: A person "does" things. The second—more contemplative, more mature and more childlike—is based upon the words of Jesus in John's Gospel: "I am the way" (John 14:6). In this second approach, Merton said, the person stops "floundering around and thrashing around and doing

84 Thomas Merton, "Monastic Spirituality: Citeaux" (Kansas City, Mo.: Credence Cassettes), tape AA 2083.

this and that."[85] One is content simply to wait for the Lord, expect the Lord and then abide in the Lord.

This Johannine approach requires a person to develop a more receptive stance towards the Divine, traditionally a characteristic of the feminine side of the soul. Perhaps this is why Saint Teresa of Avila points to the Franciscan Peter of Alcantara's statement that women make much more progress on the spiritual road than men.[86]

Women have the contemplative stance of receptivity carved into their very flesh. Men, on the other hand, are more inclined to remain on the path of "active faith." They take control in the spiritual life and *do* things. They are in charge. They tend to equate spirituality with external behavior. But this active Synoptic approach can take us only so far. To advance further along the spiritual road, we must surrender control, become receptive and have the humility to be led. We must discover and embrace the feminine aspects of our personalities in order to journey into the mysteries of the more contemplative way. Sadly, some men are just not "man enough" to do that.

Divine Care for the Trivial

In teaching us to pray for something as ordinary as bread, Jesus also teaches us that nothing is too practical or too nitty-gritty for the Father's concern. *Nothing* is inappropriate to place before God. Absolutely nothing. If it is a worry or a problem or a concern for me, then it is also a worry or a problem or a concern for God. I should not hesitate to bring it before Abba, no matter how small or trivial it may seem.

[85] Thomas Merton, "Monastic Spirituality: Part II" (Kansas City, Mo.: Credence Cassettes), tape AA 2084.
[86] *Book of Her Life*, chapter 40.

God's love has no limits; God's grace has no measure; God's concern has no boundary. Literally, God is on my side.

One afternoon, while I was preaching a mission at Saint Anthony Church in Milwaukee, Wisconsin, the parish secretary came back from her lunch hour in an exceptionally good mood. She was singing to herself and had even gone out to buy some fresh flowers for her office. I entered her office as she was arranging the flowers.

"Good afternoon, Father! I hope your day is as good as mine."

"I beg your pardon, Irene?"

"I said, 'I hope your day is as good as mine.' "

"You must have had a good lunch or something. You seem like you're on cloud nine."

She replied, "Oh, it was a great lunch! God is such a good friend to me. A special intention that I've been praying for for years has finally been answered. God takes exceptionally good care of his Irene."

"What happened, Irene?" I asked.

"Oh, now, Father, don't go prying. Some things are best kept as secrets between friends."

Whether it's something as tragic as a suicide or as trying as an unanswered prayer with Irene's "friend," we pray, "Give us this day our daily bread." We open up our hands and trust that God will provide for all our needs.

But to pray for "our daily bread" is not simply an act of childlike faith in God's providence. It is also a commitment to become daily bread for others.

The Gospels show how Jesus often broke bread with the outcasts and public sinners of his day (Mark 2:15-17). It was a consistent source of scandal and gossip: "...this fellow welcomes sinners and eats with them" (Luke 15:2). For in that act, Jesus was becoming the bread of Abba's unconditional love and forgiveness for those who had been written off by traditional religion. In his table fellowship, Jesus was making present the heavenly banquet of God's Kingdom where no one is excluded.

Almost immediately after Jesus' death and resurrection, the community of believers experienced Jesus' continuing presence and ministry around the table of fellowship. They told his story again; they received instruction and encouragement; and in the breaking of bread, they discovered not only the Lord but also their own identity and ministry (see Acts 2:42).

Become What You Receive

While preaching in Cameroon, West Africa, I heard the story of a young Christian in his twenties who had come to the village of Shisong with hopes of getting medical treatment at the small hospital staffed by the Franciscan sisters. He had the rare disease "elephantiasis." A person's extremities get exceptionally large, swollen and appear quite grotesque. In the case of this young man, it affected his right arm.

When he came to the village, no one would sell him any food. Villagers were deathly afraid of making any contact with him and wrongly feared that if they touched him or his money, they themselves would catch the disease. So they kept him at a distance from the hospital compound and the market. For two days this young man could not make his need for medicine known. He also had nothing to eat.

A Moslem in the village heard of the young Christian's plight. He went to the open village market and bought mangoes, peanuts and bananas and brought them to the young man. The Moslem did this every day in a culture where interreligious exchange on any level is still suspect and virtually taboo. One day, the young Christian said to the kind Moslem, "Sir, for the past few days, you have been my daily bread."

The bread we pray for is the same bread we are challenged to become for one another. The Moslem of Shisong intuitively understood this better than the Christians who prayed mere words at Eucharist. They had forgotten to become what they had themselves received. To receive the Bread of Life is to make the commitment to become the Bread of Life for others.

One night while travelling in mainland China in 1991, I was writing letters in the hotel room when there was a knock at the door. It was the hotel's young assistant manager who, like many Chinese, was anxious to practice his English. The small sacramentary and Mass kit left on the dresser must have given him the clue, for he addressed me as *Shenfu*, the Chinese word for "Father."

The assistant manager cautiously accepted my invitation to come in and sit down. Raising the volume on the television set so no one could overhear our conversation if the room was bugged, he began telling me about the underground Catholic Church. He detailed how he and other Chinese who remain faithful to Rome still endured blatant forms of persecution.

Realizing that we had won each other's confidence, I asked him about the student protests for democracy in Tiananmen Square in 1989. With a whisper that contained more pride than fear, he told me how this particular hotel had secretly sent vegetables and tea to help feed the protesters in Beijing. In astonishment I asked, "Wasn't that a terrible risk for this hotel?"

"Shenfu, Jesus would have commanded it," was his

matter-of-fact answer.

In China in May of 1989, the Eucharist was not housed in gold ciboriums but was carried in trucks to Tiananmen Square under the appearance of vegetables and Chinese tea.

There are so many hungry people in this world and their hunger is more than physical. Children are starving for affection. The elderly are groaning out of loneliness. People in our families and circle of friends are craving our time and attention. The poor and the sick yearn for care and understanding. The wealthy hunger for meaning. Our challenge as eucharistic people is to become the Bread of Life for others. As Saint Augustine put it: "Become what you receive." Like that Moslem and like that Chinese hotel manager, we must become the bread that feeds the hungry people around us. We are called to feed others with love, care, compassion, concern and hospitality.

That is precisely w...... we commit ourselves to at each Eucharist. The Communion distributor addresses this challenge to us personally and to the whole community: "Body of Christ." "Blood of Christ." When we say our "Amen," we accept that challenge. We say, "Yes! I am called to break my body and pour out my blood for everybody. Yes! I am daily bread for the hungry people I know and those I don't know."

That "Amen" is one of the most important words we say at Mass. We should think twice before we say it. It should make us shudder.

Barracks 26 of Dachau

On a Wednesday afternoon in June 1986, I walked the grounds of Dachau concentration camp with many other pilgrims from all over the world. I found myself almost paralyzed with grief and sorrow as I walked in stunned silence, trying to understand the Satanic horror of Nazi Germany. I remember pausing to pray at the spot where Barracks 26 once stood. It was the prison dormitory which housed so many Roman Catholics—including Gen.

Today Gen is the cook at a suburban parish in Chicago. Her experience while imprisoned in Barracks 26 speaks volumes about the meaning of the Eucharist.

Every day Catholic prisoners of Dachau got one meal which consisted of a chunk of bread the size of a dinner roll and a cup of watered-down soup. But each day, one Catholic prisoner would voluntarily sacrifice his or her meager bread ration for the celebration of Mass. That chunk of bread would be consecrated by a priest and then secretly passed around as communion for the prisoners.

That daily Eucharist in Barracks 26 of Dachau was never reduced to a pious, sentimental devotion. It was quite literally about dying to one's hunger so that others could be fed. It was about giving so that others could receive. It was, as Merton suggests, "the Sacrament of charity—that charity by which we dedicate our freedom to God and to one another."[87]

In another Nazi concentration camp, Auschwitz, Franciscan Maximilian Kolbe offered to exchange his life for that of the condemned sergeant and husband, Francis Gajowniczek. Kolbe's "eucharistic" death gives stunning witness to the words of his spiritual father, Saint Francis: "God the great Almsgiver will regard it as a theft on my part if I do not give what I have to someone who needs it more."[88]

[87] Merton, *The New Man*, p. 136.
[88] Bonaventure's *Major Life* 8:5, *Omnibus of Sources*, p. 692.

To receive the Eucharist is to make the commitment to become the Eucharist—for whomever needs it.

Broken Bread as Challenge and Mirror

Francis of Assisi challenged his followers to imitate the eucharistic action:

> Surely we cannot be left unmoved by loving sorrows for all this; in his love, God gives himself into our hands; we touch him and receive him daily into our mouths. Have we forgotten that we must fall into his hands?[89]

As Jesus has emptied himself into the hands of men and women, so we, as his disciples are called to empty ourselves into the hands of God. As Jesus has given himself totally to others, so we are called to give ourselves totally to one another.

When we do not intend to become the Eucharist for others; when we do not intend to become daily bread for another person; when we have no intention of giving ourselves totally and breaking our bodies and pouring out our blood for the salvation of this world, then the Eucharist is reduced to mere sentimentality. The Bread of Life becomes the appetizer for apathy.

Indeed, if we do not intend to "become what we receive," we would do well to absent ourselves from the communion line. "For all who eat and drink without discerning the body," Paul warned the Corinthians, "eat and drink judgment against themselves" (1 Corinthians 11:29).

Jesus challenges us with these words, "As I have broken my body and poured out my blood for you, so you are called to do this in memory of me." By virtue of our baptism, we are

---

[89] Ibid., Letter to the Clergy 8-9, p. 101.

the Body of Christ on earth. And every day, in some way, shape, or form, we are challenged to become the bread that is broken for the hungry of the world.

In the breaking of the daily eucharistic bread, we should recognize not only the Lord but also ourselves and the many times our own hearts have been broken out of love and compassion for others. The broken bread is not simply a window into the life of Jesus. It is also a mirror of our true self.

To gaze upon the Crucified is to gaze into a mirror where we see the depths of our own poverty and dependency, humility and childlikeness, charity and love. Such contemplation also leads us to rediscover who we already are: eucharistic people called to be broken for the salvation of the world.

Points for Reflection

Do I live with the illusion of independent self-sufficiency? Why does it cost me so much to admit my dependency and interior poverty?

When did I experience God as the Divine Almsgiver?

Which kind of spirituality is most dominant in my life: the active faith of the Synoptic Gospels or the contemplative childlikeness of John's Gospel?

Is my life truly "eucharistic"? How? When? Is the Eucharist a devotion or a challenge for me?

CHAPTER EIGHT

'Forgive Us Our Trespasses'

One day, Liu Lao Shr, my Chinese tutor, placed ten sentences before me and gave me the task of changing each of them into the past tense and the future tense. In the midst of the drill, I noticed an interesting gesture of hers. Whenever I was in the midst of transforming a sentence into the past tense, she would wave her hand, motioning in front of herself. And when I was transforming the sentence into the future, she would wave her hand over her shoulder, motioning behind herself. I found that curious since we Westerners think of the past being "behind" us and the future "in front" of us. So I asked her about the gesture. And sure enough, the concept of time is reversed in the Chinese mentality: The future lies *behind* us and the past is always *in front* of us.

Unfortunately, the false self sometimes grabs on to this Chinese understanding of time and forces a person to stare and obsess over a past sin.

Marie was a woman in her late sixties. I used to refer to her as the "guardian angel" of St. Raymond's parish in the Bronx. She attended daily Mass and would read or be eucharistic minister at a moment's notice. She often unlocked the church on the mornings when I overslept. Her life as a retiree also gave her the opportunity to set up and attend every funeral. Monday mornings found her counting the previous day's collection. Whenever I would thank her for her kindnesses and dedication, Marie would smile, always with a touch of sadness in her eyes, and say, "It's a way to make up for lost time." It wasn't until a year later that I discovered that her availability at the parish was, in fact, a penance she had imposed upon herself for what she believed to be "an unforgivable sin": having an abortion as a poor and pregnant nineteen-year-old woman in a small Midwestern town.

The obsession we sometimes have with our past sins is one of the worst afflictions of the soul. It transforms us into insensitive judges, rendering harsh verdicts indiscriminately. It turns us into victims of our own abuse. This obsession with the past condemns us to forced labor in a cemetery where we are repeatedly exhuming skeletons only to bury them and exhume them again. This is the death camp of the false self. And the false self can be much more demanding than God.

Listen to the prophet Micah. Filled with awe, he stands before the mercy-seat of God:

> Who is a God like you, pardoning iniquity
>   and passing over the transgression
>   of the remnant of your possession?
> He does not retain his anger forever,
>   because he delights in showing clemency.
> He will again have compassion upon us;
>   he will tread our iniquities under foot.
> You will cast all our sins
>   into the depths of the sea. (7:18-19)

Micah's God, our God, takes the sins of our past and throws them into the deepest ocean imaginable. They are gone forever. Then God places a sign over that ocean which says, "No fishing allowed." When God forgives, God forgets.

Abba's mercy sets us free from the false self's death

campaign. We are invited to be as merciful and forgiving with ourselves as Abba is with them. No matter how often we find ourselves knocking on the door of forgiveness, Abba's open arms are always waiting to carry us over the threshold.

The Divine Initiative

Jesus reveals the mercy of God. He tells us that our saving God is like the father of the prodigal son who waits at home for his beloved to return; and when he sees his child on the road, the father joyfully runs out and welcomes him back with open arms (Luke 15:11-32).

Our saving God, Jesus says, is like that anxious woman who just cannot wait until morning; in the middle of the night, she lights a lamp and very carefully sweeps the floor in hopes of finding the one lost coin (Luke 15:8-10). Our saving God is like that shepherd who leaves the ninety-nine sheep and frantically goes in search of the one lost sheep (Luke 15:1-7). Every time there is rejoicing because "what was lost has been found."

God takes the initiative and enters our sinful world bearing the alms of mercy and forgiveness. All we need do is accept what we are freely offered. We have no legal right to such mercy. We cannot earn it. We do not deserve it. Like all the things that really matter in the spiritual life, forgiveness comes as a pure gift from God.

Merton tells this story from the desert tradition of monasticism:

> An elder was asked by a certain soldier if God would forgive a sinner. And he said to him: Tell me, beloved, if your cloak is torn, will you throw it away? The soldier replied and said: No. I will mend it and put it back on. The elder said to him: If you take care of your cloak, will God not be merciful to

His own image?[90]

There is never reason to despair or doubt the forgiveness of God, no matter how hideous, heinous, or hateful the sin may be. Absolutely never. God would never destroy his own image. Recalling the spirituality of Therese of Lisieux on the feast of Christ the King, 1968, Merton told a group of religious in the Far East, *"Don't* set limits to the mercy of God. *Don't* imagine that because you are not pleasing to yourself, you're not pleasing to God."[91] According to Bonaventure, that is where Judas made his ultimate mistake. Instead of returning to the fountain of mercy out of hope for forgiveness, the disciple became terrified by the enormity of his crime and so despaired.[92]

We only need turn to God and say, "Forgive us our trespasses." And God responds with the grace of merciful forgiveness. These words of the Franciscan Anthony of Padua can be addressed to each of us, even to poor Judas: "Poor sinner, why despair of your salvation when everything speaks of love and mercy." As the beloved of Abba, we are only a heart's request from forgiveness.

The Transformation of Francis of Assisi

Young Francis of Assisi must have been a man steeped in shame and guilt. Celano's first biography of the saint gives evidence of a very sinful past for which Francis needed to repent. And Francis did. He sought out a place of prayer one day at Poggio Bustone and reflected upon all the good things

[90] Merton, *The Wisdom of the Desert*, p. 76.

[91] Thomas Merton, "Sanctity" (Kansas City, Mo.: Credence Cassettes),tape AA 2459.

[92] *Tree of Life* 20, in *Bonaventure: The Soul's Journey into God. The Tree of Life. The Life of Saint Francis*, trans. by Ewert Cousins (Mahwah, N.J.: Paulist Press, 1978).

God was doing through him and all the gifts God had given to him.

While reflecting upon these alms with the gratitude of adoration, Francis simultaneously was aware of the abomination of his sins. He started praying, "O God, be merciful to me the sinner." As he prayed that prayer, Celano writes, "there was poured into Francis a certainty that all his sins had been forgiven and a confidence of his restoration to grace was given him." At that moment, Francis experienced the alms of God's merciful forgiveness in a way he never before had experienced. He accepted what was given him from the throne of grace: the awareness that God took the initiative, entered into his sinfulness and stretched out the hand of salvation to a drowning man. All had been forgiven and forgotten. There no longer was need to brood over his past. Celano concludes the narration of this event with a telling remark: "[R]enewed in spirit, [Francis] seemed changed into another man."[93]

The love of God continually entices us to renounce illusions of the false self, to turn around and come back home to our true self. Since mercy is a dimension of Divine love, it should come as no surprise that Francis was renewed and transformed by this experience. Asking for pardon is realizing that sin is not written with indelible ink. We are not condemned to living with the past in front of us, staring us in the face. We are not left to drown in the chaos created by the false self.

Marie's abortion was an albatross around her neck. Her years of self-inflicted penance simply fed her shame. Her entire spiritual life and personal piety were anchored in the guilt of her sin. She often told me that she was afraid God

---

[93] Celano's *First Life* 26, *Omnibus of Sources*, p. 250.

was going to throw it up in her face on Judgment Day. "God cannot forgive something so terrible. I'll have to answer for it and I won't know what to say."

On many occasions Marie and I talked about the Abba of Jesus and how this God forgives and forgets. I tried to take different approaches, yet each time I would run up against the brick wall of Marie's guilt. No argument, no matter its craft or ingenuity, could break through the prison which the false self had erected around Marie's soul.

One Saturday afternoon before the vigil Mass, I noticed Marie sitting in her favorite location: the pew before the side altar dedicated to the Sacred Heart. I went up to greet her and ask her to "whisper a prayer for me" as I always did. She looked up and smiled. But something was different. There was no sadness in her eyes. She did not even give her usual response, "And you do the same for me." Instead, she replied, "I'd be delighted to, Father!"

I had the six o'clock Mass the following morning—and I overslept. I got to the sacristy about fifteen minutes before Mass only to discover that, for the first time since I had been at St. Raymond's, Marie had not unlocked the church.

Over the following weeks, Marie continued to attend daily Mass, but she suddenly asked not to read anymore. She said it made her nervous. She still helped out with funeral preparations, but she stopped counting the collections on Mondays. "A woman my age should be enjoying the morning talk shows on television," she said.

Something happened between the Sacred Heart and Marie on that Saturday afternoon. She once hinted at it but never volunteered the facts. I suspect she had an experience of God's merciful arms wrapped around her as she stared through the prison bars into her past. That was all it took to break the false self's lock.

'The Open Bosom of Divine Mercy'

Bonaventure uses the vivid image of a bosom to describe the mercy of God. "The Good Shepherd extended fatherly affection to the repentant, showing the open bosom of Divine mercy."[94] "Bosom"—it can mean a mother's breasts, the very place an infant finds life-giving milk and nourishment. But "bosom" also connotes the very center of a man's chest, symbolizing strength and security. Bonaventure's image incorporates both the masculine and feminine dimensions of Divine forgiveness.

As proof of the Divine mercy of the Good Shepherd, Bonaventure calls upon four witnesses from the Gospels: Matthew, Zacchaeus, the sinful woman who washed the feet of Jesus with her tears, and the woman caught in adultery. Each of these witnesses saw and took nourishment from the open bosom of Divine mercy. And each, like Francis of Assisi and Marie, was changed into another person.

Matthew was collecting taxes when he encountered the Good Shepherd (Matthew 9:9-13). He must have been stunned by Jesus' simple invitation: "Follow me." This meticulous tax collector, whose preoccupation centered upon adding up debits, was standing before Jesus, the shepherd of forgiveness who only knew subtraction. Matthew could respond in only one way. "...[H]e got up and followed [Jesus]." Matthew's life changed drastically. So did the lives of so many of the poor for whom Matthew's calling meant a cancellation of their tax debts. In touching one person, God's mercy often affects others.

Zacchaeus's conversion had its roots in his curiosity (Luke 19:1-10). Also a tax collector, he climbed a sycamore tree to get a peek at this man Jesus about whom he had heard

---

[94] *Tree of Life* 13.

so much. But the Good Shepherd was not content simply to let Zacchaeus satisfy his curiosity. So Jesus took the initiative and shook Zacchaeus out of his tree with words of love and anticipation: "Come down quickly!"

Zacchaeus was as stunned as the crowd which grumbled at the Master going to the house of a sinner. But Zacchaeus also saw a ray of light guiding him out of his past criminal extortions, and he responded to Jesus with the promise of amends. He then shared his daily bread with the Good Shepherd. Sometimes we know what we want; we just need someone to give us the practical encouragement and added push.

The sinful woman of Luke's Gospel (7:36-50) was so aware of the abomination of her sinfulness before the open bosom of Divine mercy that she wept at the feet of Jesus. Her conscience demanded that she prove the depths of her heart's contrition. But her past life had taught her only one way to relate to men. So she touched the Lord, washing his feet with her tears, her kisses and her costly ointment.

The touch itself was enough. Jesus understood. The Good Shepherd said to her, "Your sins are forgiven. Your faith has saved you. Go in peace."

The woman caught in adultery (John 8:3-11)—one can only imagine her fear and shame as her sin was paraded before the entire city. The Mosaic law stated her sentence clearly: death by stoning.

There was no need for a judge in this case. Yet the scribes and Pharisees brought her before Jesus to have her sentence of death confirmed. And what does the Good Shepherd say? "I do not condemn you. Go, and from now on, do not sin anymore." This woman was nourished by the milk of God's forgiveness as she nursed at the open bosom of Divine mercy.

Bonaventure concludes his reflection on the mercy and forgiveness of the Good Shepherd with an exhortation which summarizes the attitudes of those four Gospel witnesses who experienced the fatherly affection of Jesus and his open bosom of Divine mercy. He writes:

> Like Matthew, therefore
> follow this most devoted shepherd;
> like Zacchaeus
> receive him with hospitality;
> like the sinful woman
> anoint him with ointment
> and wash his feet with your tears,
> wipe them with your hair
> and caress them with your kisses,
> so that finally,
> with the woman presented to him for judgment,
> you may deserve to hear
> the sentence of forgiveness:
> "Has no one condemned you? Neither will I condemn you.
> Go, and sin no more."[95]

When we pray, "Forgive us our trespasses" in the Lord's Prayer, we stand in line with Matthew, Zacchaeus, the sinful woman and the woman caught in adultery. With these great Gospel witnesses, we too can experience the power of Divine forgiveness as Abba forgets the past, puts the future back in front of us and welcomes us home to the present moment with wide-opened merciful arms.

Points for Reflection

What sins of my past does the false self insist upon placing in front of me? Why? Why do I struggle to

[95] Ibid., p. 137.

believe in God's forgiveness?

Do I set limits upon the mercy of God?

Of Bonaventure's four Gospel witnesses to the Good Shepherd's forgiveness, with whom do I identify the most?

CHAPTER NINE

'As We Forgive Those Who Trespass Against Us'

I t happened on my vacation in June of 1981 as I introduced another friar to the sights and sounds of my hometown, New Orleans. We boarded the St. Charles Avenue streetcar at the beginning of the line and then rolled down Carrollton Avenue. To this day I still do not know what possessed me to get off the streetcar at the Oak Street stop. But we did.

I had not walked down Oak Street since my father's suicide in 1968. But even after thirteen years, so much of it remained the same. The big blue and white sign still proclaimed "Haase's Shoe Store." I remembered being ten, eleven and twelve years old and taking the St. Charles streetcar to Oak Street to surprise my father with a visit after school. I remembered how my father would take me into his office that overlooked the sales area of the store. I remembered the pet parakeet and how I would spend endless hours trying to get that bird to say "Welcome to Haase's."

I had not been in the store since my father's funeral. At the news of his sudden and tragic death, each side of the family pointed a finger of blame at the other. As a result, I had not seen my father's side of the family or the shoestore for thirteen years. My father's sister, my aunt Vera May, still owned and managed the shoestore. As my friend and I passed the store, I suddenly felt drawn to go in. I was scared. I had not seen my aunt for over a decade. And frankly, I did not know if I wanted to see her now. But within a matter of seconds, I found myself inside my father's store. A salesman, later revealed to be one of my cousins, approached and asked if he could help me.

I must have looked foolish. I just stood there and finally blurted out that I wanted to see my aunt.

Within a few minutes, I heard steps coming down the stairs. There she stood. Aunt Vera May. From a distance we stared at each other: She, probably trying to figure out who I was, and I, gazing upon her face as if my father had suddenly come alive. Within a split second, she recognized me. And with that, the gift was given instantly. It was the blossom of two broken hearts. Forgiveness. Mercy.

For the first time in thirteen years, my aunt and I embraced, shed tears of sorrow and regret, and held one another. It was then that I discovered something which I should have known all along. The pain of my father's death, which had consumed me for all those years, was just as real for my aunt. She too had loved my father. I discovered then and there the ugliness and lie of holding grudges: They strip the other person of a human heart.

My friend Dan just stood there. When it finally dawned on him what he had just witnessed, he signed himself with the cross. And maybe that is the best response to a moment of forgiveness: to call to mind the crucified Christ who forgave his own persecutors as he hung upon the cross.

The Revolution of Forgiveness

Of all the teachings of Jesus, it was his teaching on forgiving one's neighbor that turned a doctrine of traditional

Judaism upside down. Traditional Judaism saw revenge, as long as it was equitable, as a way of insuring that justice was done: "Eye for eye, tooth for tooth" (Exodus 21:24). This is the way the Hebrew Scriptures describe a revenge that is just and balanced.

Then came Jesus. He challenged this traditional understanding of revenge—and caused a revolution in our thinking about forgiveness. Jesus taught that authentic forgiveness is not a business deal. Like charity, forgiveness is given totally for free, with no strings attached. He insisted that justice is served not by settling accounts or getting revenge but by generously sharing with others what we ourselves have experienced in the alms of God. "Just as the Lord has forgiven you, so you also must forgive" (Colossians 3:13b). Forgiving our neighbor is our response to God's forgiveness.

To refuse forgiveness is to demand more from another person than God has demanded of us. Jesus has strong words for those who practice this kind of injustice: "But if you do not forgive others, neither will the Father forgive your trespasses" (Matthew 6:15). More so, in the parable of the unforgiving servant, he states that this kind of hypocritical injustice makes us loan sharks liable for punishment:

> "You wicked slave! I forgave you all that debt because you pleaded with me. Should you not have had mercy on your fellow slave, as I had mercy on you?" And in anger his lord handed him over to be tortured until he would pay his entire debt. So my heavenly Father will also do to every one of you, if you do not forgive your brother or sister from your heart. (Matthew 18:32-35)

We cannot proclaim God as a Father of forgiveness in prayer unless we proclaim God as a Father of forgiveness by the way we live our lives—by the way "we forgive those who have trespassed against us."

When we refuse to forgive someone, we are like the elder son in the prodigal son parable (Luke 15:28): We remain slaves to the false self, obeying the commands of a bruised ego. We become prisoners of our own hearts.

The Mechanics of Forgiveness

Along with an international group of friars travelling in China, I went to meet a Chinese bishop and fellow Franciscan. (His name and location must remain confidential to insure his safety.) A member of the Franciscan Order before the Communist takeover, this bishop was arrested in the late 1940's. He was sentenced to make umbrella handles in one of his own churches which had been turned into a factory for the People's Republic of China. His treatment was less than humane.

With the changing political winds in China in the late 1980's, this bishop was released and restored to his diocese under the direction of the government-sponsored Patriotic Association of the Chinese Catholic Church, which is permitted no ties to Rome. By the time of our visit, the Chinese government suspected he had been secretly legitimized by Rome as the local episcopal ordinary, and so this elderly bishop was being continually harassed and interrogated. Two months before our visit, he had been awakened in the middle of the night, brought to a local police station and questioned intensely for some ten hours.

When he was led into the parlor by his government-appointed "assistant," he greeted us with the traditional Franciscan salutation in Latin, "Pax et bonum!" ("Peace and good things!"). Though small in stature, he exuded a bold, yet self-effacing, spirit. His large round eyes radiated an inner peace and contentment.

We spoke through a translator, but I could tell the bishop took an instant liking to me—perhaps because I dropped all episcopal etiquette and called him by the Latin religious name he held in the Order.

I asked him directly, "Frater B., are you angry at what has happened to you?"

"Frater Albertus," he said, "to dwell on the many times people have slapped me on the cheek is simply to prolong the pain of my—" He hesitated for the word. He looked at the government translator out of the corner of his eyes, and then continued, "—the pain of my *hospitalization*. I have decided not to give my *doctors* that much enjoyment."

Like a true follower of Francis of Assisi, Frater B. refused to let his past history of forced labor scar him for life and fill him with rancor. He renounced the false self's temptation to let the anger and bitterness stick. Consequently, there was no "edge" to his personality. His large peaceful eyes witnessed to the sincerity of his words.

Frater B. had decided to let the hurt go.

It takes a lot of emotional and psychological energy to keep a wound open, to keep a grudge alive. And the more I work to keep it alive, the more emotionally drained I become as the grudge saps me of my strength. The longer I allow a wound to fester, or the longer I keep picking its scab, the more bitterness, anger and self-pity poison my blood and eat at my heart.

Some people seem to have a "velcro personality" to which all hurts stick: "Five years, four months, and two days ago, so-and-so did this to me!" Treasured emotional wounds and scars become like fish bones stuck in the throat. Even the smallest bone can be excruciating—and the more one struggles to unstick it, the more it hurts.

Others seem to have the good fortune of a "teflon personality" and all hurts seem to slide right off. But the "teflon" is the result of a *decision* to let the hurt go. These personalities dump it into the ocean of the past. They stop picking the scab.

Forgiving With Our Eyes

Eyes shed a lot of light upon the condition of a person's heart. Jesus himself called our eyes "the lamp of the body" (Matthew 6:22). They can blaze with anger; they can be as peaceful as an evening sunset; they can dance with excitement and passion; they can soothe with the balm of mercy and kindness.

Francis says that those who need to be forgiven should discover mercy "in your eyes." In a letter written to an anonymous Provincial Minister, Francis offered some advice on how to deal with friars who sin publicly:

> [T]here should not be any brother in the world who has sinned, however much he may have possibly sinned, who, after he has looked into your eyes, would go away without having received your mercy, if he is looking for mercy. And if he were not to seek mercy, you should ask him if he wants mercy. And if he should sin thereafter a thousand times before your very eyes, love him more than me so that you may draw him back to the Lord. Always be merciful to brothers such as these.[96]

Our forgiving eyes should offer a refuge to those frantic people who, like the sinful woman of Luke's Gospel (7:36-50), crave forgiveness but never learned the social grace of asking for it. But, as Francis suggests, even the poorest beggar has learned the art of reading another's eyes:

[96] *Francis and Clare*, p. 74.

no one "after looking into your eyes" should be denied finding mercy, "if he is looking for mercy." And what an abundant alms it is to preserve the dignity of people and offer them forgiveness with our eyes when life, for whatever reason, has robbed them of the ability to ask for it with words.

Sometimes people live through the wounds, scars and pain of their brokenness. Charity demands that we try to become aware of the wound out of which they may be living—even when their brokenness inflicts hurts on us. To be sensitive to the hurt of another's heart is to gain an insight into what makes that person tick.

In trying to understand the hearts of people and confronting others with compassion, we sometimes discover that what we thought was intentional was never really intended in the first place. But even if the harm is intended, Francis challenges believers to offer mercy and forgiveness—and "a thousand times" if need be!

Don't let the hurt stick and become a grudge. Leave the past in the past. Come back home to the present.

Deciding to let go of a hurt is not a matter of "forgiving and forgetting"—as we are often told so glibly. In forgiving my neighbor, *I remember*—but I choose not to fuss over the past! I remember, but I choose not to become entangled in the tentacles of a grudge. Frater B. didn't forget, but he made the conscious decision not to drink the vinegar of revenge and bitterness. That is the evening cocktail of the false self.

The Dynamite of Grace

Some hurts strike so deeply that we feel unable to forgive. We begin drowning in resentment, bitterness, anger. Sometimes we truly want to forgive, yet seem unable to find the emotional strength to do so.

What do we do when we want to move beyond the hurt, when we want to forgive, but we just don't know how? We can find a solution in the famous incident narrated by Corrie ten Boom in her book, *The Hiding Place*.

Corrie ten Boom lived in Amsterdam during World War II. Because her family was caught sheltering Jews, she and her sister Betsy were sent to the infamous Ravensbruck concentration camp. Only Corrie survived.

After the war, Corrie ten Boom committed herself to a life of lecturing. She traveled throughout Europe speaking on the topic of forgiveness and reconciliation.

One day after giving her talk in Munich, Germany, a man came forward to thank her for the talk. Corrie couldn't believe her eyes. He was one of the Nazi guards who used to stand duty in the women's shower room at Ravensbruck.

The man reached out to shake Corrie's hand, but she froze. After all her talks on forgiveness, she could not reach out her hand in friendship. Her physical body remembered too sharply the horror of the camp and the death of her beloved sister. Corrie was blocked emotionally, stuck in the crippling and debilitating rut of resentment, bitterness, hatred.

As Corrie stood there, frozen with shock, the battle raged inside of her. She was torn between the seductive desire to balance the scales of justice with violence and revenge and to heed Jesus' challenge of forgiveness which she herself had preached so often. So she prayed silently to herself, "Jesus, I cannot forgive this man. Give me your forgiveness."

And as she prayed that prayer and as her mind's eye reviewed the years of brutality, suffering, humiliation, death, her hand suddenly lifted from her side! This former prisoner found herself offering the former shower guard the one thing she thought she did not know how to give. "I forgive you, brother, with all my heart!"

Corrie ten Boom's experience reminds us that forgiveness is not simply a matter of choice, of making a decision. It is also a grace from God—the "eighth gift" of the Holy Spirit. And we have to be willing to pray for it: "Jesus, I cannot forgive this person. Give me your forgiveness." Willpower and personal desire are not always enough to break through the wall of resentment and bitterness built around the heart by the false self. We sometimes need the dynamite of God's grace.

And it will come. It might come like lightning as in Corrie's case. It might take years as it did with my aunt and me. So we pray for the grace to forgive those who trespass against us patiently, lovingly, confidently.

Inner Healing

When I meet people in spiritual direction who are stuck in the rut of bitterness or who seem particularly attached to a certain past hurt or injustice, I ask them two questions: What are you gaining by keeping this grudge alive? What need is it satisfying in you?

Our desire for revenge or self-pity and our need to hold on to a grudge are sometimes the tip of an iceberg that runs deep down inside of us. One has to get below the surface of the self-pity and emotional need for justice in order to find out what are the deeper issues manifested in the grudge or desire for revenge. In other words, some grudges are actually pointing to deeper aspects of one's personality which have yet to be faced and integrated.

In the parable of the prodigal son, the elder son's anger and refusal to enter his brother's homecoming party were actually manifestations of a much deeper wound. The elder son told his father:

> Listen! For all these years I have been working like a slave for you, and I have never disobeyed your command.... But when this son of yours came back, who has devoured your property with prostitutes, you kill the fatted calf for him! (Luke 15:29-30)

The elder son never felt accepted, appreciated or loved by his father. That was the real issue. Furthermore, he had been continually frustrated in his attempts to earn his father's approval, attention and affection. And so his resentment towards his younger brother was really pointing to a deeper wound: He felt like a forgotten orphan; he did not feel beloved.

What are you gaining by keeping a grudge alive? What need is it satisfying in you? Answers to these questions often reveal fundamental wounds out of which many people live their lives and the very reason they react to others out of bitterness and malice. The hostility directed toward others is really a projection of one's inner wound.

Lack of self-love, the absence of a loving parent during one's formative years, the scars of sexual abuse, living in the shadow of a more talented sibling—these are wounds that never really heal. Just like the wounds still visible on the Risen Christ, some have so shaped our present identity that they remain with us forever. Yet, also like the wounds of the Risen Christ, these wounds *do stop bleeding*. They no longer drain us of our emotional and psychological energies. They no longer condemn us to our past. By the grace of God, they become our marks of victory and the very signs of God's healing power in our lives. They become proclamations that "death has been swallowed up in victory" (1 Corinthians 15:54). "[I]f we have been united with [Christ] in a death like his, we will certainly be united with him in a resurrection like his" (Romans 6:5).

The wounds of crucifixion dry up and are transformed into the marks of resurrection the moment my desire for revenge is converted into the balm of mercy and forgiveness. That change—or emotional "shift"—often occurs through the grace of an insight. Sometimes a person arrives at that insight through some form of inner healing: psychotherapy, prayer, membership in twelve-step support groups, dialogue with a loved one or a trusted friend. I often suggest to those I counsel that they develop their own personal method of inner healing based upon five important principles: the continuing presence of a loving, compassionate Christ; a review of the past event; the "step of compassion"; calling upon the healing ministry of Christ; and the proclamation of new life.

The continuing presence of a loving, compassionate Christ. The first principle of inner healing is that it is always done in the presence of Jesus the Divine Physician. He is the one who heals, comforts and consoles. The Jesus who wept at the news of Lazarus's death is the same compassionate Jesus who ministers to us. He has an investment in our broken hearts. "The Lord is near to the brokenhearted, and saves the crushed in spirit" (Psalm 34:18). "[God] heals the brokenhearted, and binds up their wounds" (Psalm 147:3). We must trust that as we approach any method of inner healing.

A review of the past event. We must go back to the past event and take another look at it. This is the hardest task of inner healing because we tend to live our lives "around" our wounds, evading our hurts, skirting our scars. We rarely, if ever, confront them head on.

Mary has a fine reputation among the members of her

congregation. In public, she appears organized, upbeat and fun-loving. But the people who live with her see a very different side of Mary: troubled, lethargic, verging on alcoholism, constantly drained. Mary has spent most of her life refusing to confront some deep emotional issues which are probably centered around her mother whom she never talks about. Mary is living her life "around" her wound.

Our external behaviors often betray the fact that we are running away from something or actively repressing something. Sex, alcohol, workaholic busyness, uncontrollable anger—these are not usually the real problems. They are what we are doing *about* the problems. The process of inner healing is delving below the manifestation of the problem to get to the problem itself. We get rid of weeds by pulling them up by their roots. We confront the past head-on.

Many will charge that "dragging up the past" is fruitless and wastes time on things that are best forgotten. But we must remember that emotional wounds are like physical wounds: They do not heal if they are neglected; they only become infected. The hurt must be brought into the light of the sun and treated. It demands to be recognized.

This does not mean, however, that all wounds can—or should—be confronted *now*. We must not violate ourselves and force ourselves to confront issues or events which we are not ready to face. To do so is to promote the mentality of the false self.

Healing is not an achievement; it is a gift. When the time is right, the memory will "perk up" to the surface. That is a sign that it is time to begin the healing process. In the meantime, Abba has given us our defense mechanisms precisely so that we can protect ourselves from the very issues or wounds that we are not yet ready to confront. Joan's tragedy offers a vivid example.

At an early age, Joan had been sexually abused by her father. For twenty-six years she had repressed that abuse. At age thirty, she fell in love with Bill. At times she began to feel "uncomfortable" during their relationship but didn't quite know why. She often projected those "uncomfortable" feelings upon Bill. These mixed signals strained their relationship. Then dreams began, and Joan would awaken to feelings of stress and anxiety. Finally came conscious flashbacks to the past incident with her father. The wound was "perking up." It was calling for attention and healing. It was time to face the past abuse.

Healing begins with the journey through the memory to the past—but in the presence of the Risen Christ. We must allow ourselves to enter again into the darkness of the betrayal, the abuse, the hurt, the wound. We expose the entire incident to the light shining through the wounds of the Risen Christ. We recall the details of the experience and the feelings it raised inside of us. At this point, verbalizing the experience to a caring friend or someone in the helping professions can be of utmost value.

The "step of compassion." The third step of inner healing is the "step of compassion" when we momentarily step through our pain, anger and hurt to place our feet in the shoes of the betrayer, to understand the heart of the betrayer. This is precisely what the father of the prodigal son encouraged his elder son to do in order to break through his resentment: "[W]e had to celebrate and rejoice, because this brother of yours was dead and has come to life; he was lost and has been found" (Luke 15:32).Understanding breeds forgiveness.

Several questions help in that process of understanding our betrayer. Out of what emotional wound was the betrayer living? What pain filled the heart of the betrayer that would cause a person to react to us or treat us in the way the betrayer did? How emotionally healthy is the betrayer? An insight will sometimes plant itself within our souls as we try to understand the betrayer's heart, as we walk in the shoes of the one who betrayed us, as we enter into the flames of the betrayer's hell.

Only when we understand the weaknesses and imperfections of others can we forgive them with humility and compassion—the two virtues Thomas Merton believes are essential to Christian forgiveness. He writes:

> If we forgive [others] without humility, our forgiveness is a mockery: it presupposes that we are better than they. Jesus descended into the abyss of our degradation in order to forgive us after He had, in a sense, become lower than us all. It is not for us to forgive others from lofty thrones, as if we were gods looking down on them from Heaven. We must forgive them in the flames of their own hell, for Christ, by means of our forgiveness, once again descends to extinguish the avenging flame. He cannot do this if we do not forgive others with His own compassion.[97]

The wound left by my father's suicide began to dry up as I became more and more aware that Dad was probably doing the best he could on that day. If he could have done better, he probably would have. But on October 22, 1968, that was all he was capable of. And Joan began to be relieved of some of the trauma of her early sexual abuse as she grew in the realization of her father's emotional sickness.

Inner healing begins when we realize that most of the time, most people were doing the best they could. Sadly, the people who shape our broken personalities are broken

---

[97] Thomas Merton, *No Man Is an Island* (Garden City, N.Y.: Image Books, 1967), p. 163.

themselves. Does that brokenness exonerate them from the trauma or injury they inflicted upon us? Does that absolve or vindicate adults who deliberately betray our trust? No. The "step of compassion" has but one single purpose: to walk in the shoes of the betrayer in order to realize that crippled people cannot walk without a limp. And life being as it is, we are all limping.

Calling upon the healing ministry of Christ. After we have lived through the experience again in the presence of the Risen Christ and tried to understand the heart of the betrayer, we can then take the next step to inner healing: We turn to Jesus and ask him to minister to us.

The Risen Christ is both the physician and the balm. We allow the healing light that shines through his glorified wounds to penetrate the deep recesses and caverns of our broken hearts. The power "flowing from Jesus' resurrection" (Philippians 3:10)will often burn away the false self's need to crusade, to be vindicated, to be justified, to have revenge. And through Christ's healing touch, light appears where darkness once prevailed. Life comes forth as he calls down the wounds of our past, "Come out!"

Sometimes, even after life is restored, there is work to be done. After raising Lazarus, Jesus said to those standing by, "Unbind him, and let him go" (John 11:44).In restoring life to those areas in our past which have so wounded us or caused us deep emotional pain, Jesus often enlists the help of others to unbind us. Thus inner healing often is accompanied by professional counseling, spiritual direction and membership in support groups.

The proclamation of new life. Over time and through the grace of inner healing, the wounds of the past begin to dry up. They no longer drain us of our emotional energy. The infections of anger, bitterness and self-pity gradually fade from our lives. Though we cannot help but look at the world through the wounds and hurts which have shaped us, we begin to realize that it is not nearly as hostile as we originally thought.

An emotional "shift" occurs. We begin to walk on equal ground with other broken people who are sometimes in need of our forgiveness *again*. We also find ourselves reaching through our wound to extend a helping hand of compassion to those suffering the same pain or hurt that we once endured.

The final step of healing comes when we can announce our own new life. When someone asks, "Where is that young boy whose life was shattered by his beloved father's suicide?" or, "Where is that bitter, distrusting woman who was sexually violated by the very parent she so innocently trusted?" or, "Where is that person who was so severely scarred by divorce?" or, "Where is that man who hated himself?," we reply with the angels at the tomb on Easter morning, "Why do you look for the living among the dead? He is not here, but has risen" (Luke 24:5b-6).

When we pray for the courage and grace to forgive those who trespass against us in the Lord's Prayer, we are also committing ourselves to share in the healing dimension of Christ's resurrection: the proclamation that a deeper experience of Abba's unconditional love and mercy exists despite the hurts and wounds inflicted upon us by others.

Points for Reflection

Is there a person whom I refuse to forgive? Why? What am I gaining by keeping that grudge alive? What need is it satisfying in me?

In a recent act of forgiveness, what did I learn about my betrayer?

When did I experience someone forgiving me "with their eyes"? How did I react to that?

How have I experienced the healing power of Christ's resurrection in my own process of inner healing?

CHAPTER TEN

'Lead Us Not Into Temptation'

We have all experienced temptation. We're tempted to keep our mouths shut and not tell the lady at the drugstore that she gave us a dollar too much in change. We're tempted sexually. We're tempted to ignore the outstretched hand begging for loose change. We're tempted to tell a little white lie for the sake of our pride or reputation. We're tempted to remain silent before the injustices committed against the poor and powerless. We're tempted to lash out with angry, violent words against those closest to us. Temptation wears many hats and comes in different degrees, but by its very nature, it's always enticing and seductive.

Rationalization is the bridge from the land of temptation to the desert of apathy, evil, sin:

- "The cashier at the drugstore should be more careful when giving change. If she wants to give me an extra dollar, I'll take it!"

- "If that poor fellow went out and got a job like me, he wouldn't have to beg for money on the streetcorner."

- "I can't be bothered with writing a letter to my senator. After all, we live in the United States, not Central America!"

Rationalization is the thinking process which fuels the illusion and deception of the false self. It is a trap set by the power of evil.

What is this "power of evil"? Thomas Merton told the young monks of Gethsemani that he doubted if the devil had a tail, horns, or carried a pitchfork. But he added, "...behind the attractions and the surface of things in the world, there *is* a force at work to deceive people—a force of deception." Language is inadequate to describe this force yet, Merton stated bluntly, "Something's cooking.... And look out!... If you stay out of the way of this force—whatever it is—you are better off. And if you go horsing around with it, you are in trouble."[98]

Rationalization is a way of "horsing around" with the reality of evil. The process of thinking promoted by the false self and the power of evil is coldly logical and cruelly detached from emotion. Merton says that the decision to fire nuclear weapons will be made by "sane people" who "have *perfectly good reasons*, logical, well-adjusted reasons, for firing the shot. They will be obeying sane orders that have come sanely down the chain of command.... When the missiles take off, then, *it will be no mistake.*"[99]

How often do we find ourselves trying to come up with a reason for doing something that we know in our hearts is wrong? How often do we find ourselves doing all kinds of mental gymnastics in order to justify something—"sane" as it may be—that is steeped in the selfishness and pure logic of the false self? Whenever we do, the music has started playing and the slow dance of temptation has begun. "Lead us not into the tempation of sinful rationalization."

A friar once confessed to me that he is more embarrassed by his temptations than by his sin. That is a keen insight. To

[98] Thomas Merton, "The Patience of Conversion" (Kansas City, Mo.: Credence Cassettes), tape AA 2232.
[99] Thomas Merton, "A Devout Meditation in Memory of Adolf Eichmann," in *Raids on the Unspeakable* (New York: New Directions, 1964), p. 47.

sin takes a split second. It is the heart's dive into the pool of deliberate weakness and willed imperfection. We usually spend a lot more time planning the dive, "horsing around" with the temptation.

The way we mull over our temptations and fine-tune our arguments for acting upon them are indications that we actually enjoy the dance with the devil. The way we poke around various temptations, like hunters checking to see if the animal is really dead, reveals our continuing attraction and fascination with the swaggering excitement of the false self's agenda.

The Idolatry of the 'Eight P's'

There are temptations, and there is Temptation!

Little white lies. Apathy and indifference towards our brothers or sisters. Sexual temptations. They are all temptations with a small "t." They are real. They occur every day of our lives. They tempt us to promote the logic of the false self through rationalization and justification. The more we respond to them, the more they become second nature to us.

But there is also temptation with a capital "T." It is the great temptation: the primordial temptation of Jews and Christians to worship a false god. This too is the "temptation" we pray not to be "led into" in the Lord's Prayer.

Idolatry is so very seductive. Its trap is set very early in life and most of us get caught in it, though few of us are aware of having done so.

I fall prey to worshiping a false god because society, upbringing or friends tell me there is something missing or lacking in my life. Whatever it might be, I am told that "this missing thing will make you happy." So I develop a taste for it. I crave it. I desire it with all my heart. I go after it. I become obsessed with getting it, having it, keeping it and accumulating more of it. My life revolves around it. When I have it, I tell myself that I am happy and that life is going well. When I don't have it, I tell myself that I am unhappy. I am its slave.

Power, prestige, people, possessions, productivity, popularity, pleasure and position—these are the golden calves of the twentieth century. These "eight P's" are the "it" we need to be happy. Without the "eight P's," we're nothing. We're failures. And so, like Adam and Eve, we keep reaching out to pluck these "eight P's," convinced they will bring us happiness and peace.

We all know power-hungry people. They have to have power, control and mastery over your life, my life and everybody else's life. These are the people who have an emotional need to be king of the hill or queen for a day, seven days a week—and they will not be happy until they are. Their false god is power.

We all know people who act like peacocks. Masters and mistresses of the grand entrance, they crave prestige and position. Like power-hungry people, they will lie, cheat and back-bite in order to get the promotion or be appointed to some special position. They love to see their names in lights. They go after more and more honor, glory and praise. And the more they have, the more they want. They are never content. Their every move proclaims the words of the bumper-sticker on my bedroom door, "We'll get along fine as soon as you realize I AM GOD." Their idols are prestige and position.

Some people try to boost their poor self-images with the passing happiness of possessions. The more "stuff" these people have, the more secure and attractive they think they are. Their self-worth is tied up in the external objects which newspapers and television claim are the measures of happiness and success: big houses, fancy cars, expensive jewelry, fashionable clothes. There is nothing wrong with these things, but people who worship possessions go after them thinking they equal abundant life. Consequently, they become possessed by their own possessions.

Workaholics worship productivity. Merton describes them:

> The soul that projects itself entirely into activity, and seeks itself outside itself in the work of its own will is like a madman who sleeps on the sidewalk in front of his house instead of living inside where it is quiet and warm. The soul that throws itself outdoors in order to find itself in the effects of its own work is like a fire that has no desire to burn but seeks only to go up in smoke.[100]

Though always verging on exhaustion, these people keep cranking out the work so that others will admire them, like them, respect them, and most of all, need them. Sometimes obsessed with a success measured by report cards, progress reports or yearly evaluations, they forget to live.

When sickness or mandatory retirement forces these people to stop working, they feel as if life has come to an end. Why? Because they feel useless and worthless. Their self-worth and self-esteem are tied up in what they do, not in who they are.

The lonely people of the world really and truly believe that some person will cure all their restlessness and anxiety. A more caring spouse or one more friend, they think, will ease their dissatisfaction and unhappiness. More than one couple has made the tragic decision to have another child in

[100] Merton, *No Man Is an Island*, p. 98.

hopes of solving the "seven-year itch" in marriage. Unfortunately, the child becomes a pawn between two unhappy people. People are not solutions to our emotional problems.

During his four years as a Franciscan, Tony was a very close friend of mine. The immediate rapport between us blossomed into a wonderful and caring friendship. Naturally, I was hurt when he called that February evening and told me he was leaving the Order. I felt betrayed. I was angry. I wanted to keep him from leaving because I knew that, once he left, our friendship would change. And it did.

We lost contact for four years. Then while preaching a parish mission in the city where Tony was living, I called him on the phone. Within minutes, we made arrangements to go out to dinner that evening. And before I knew it, we were sitting together in a restaurant enjoying each other's company again.

That evening Tony answered a question left unasked for four years. "Why did you leave the Order?"

He answered bluntly. He could not find meaning in the pain of celibacy. He said that the loneliness would sometimes crush him at night. He said, "As much as I loved the Order and what it stands for, I came to realize that I needed a wife more."

After he left the Order, Tony got a job with one of the "Big Ten" accounting firms in Cleveland. Within a year he had met a woman, fallen in love, and was currently sharing an apartment with her.

"Judy and I have been together now for some two and a half years and yet, Albert, I'm still not happy. I'm just not satisfied. And that is beginning to cause some frustration in my relationship with Judy. I think I know why. I guess I've been asking her to do the impossible for me."

He hit the nail on the head. Tony had made the classic mistake that so many people make in marriage. One spouse expects the other "to make me happy."

People who worship pleasure are in constant search of another emotional high that will give them a quick fix. Out of desperation or sheer boredom, these thrill-seekers search out forms of diversion and entertainment that can often trigger addiction or develop into unhealthy compulsions: alcohol, sex, drugs, romance, gambling, food.

Pleasure-worshipers have an emotional need for constant excitement and stimulation. Every day of their lives must be spectacular and upbeat. Sadly, these people live a vicious cycle of frustration: to have a thrill fulfilled is simply to deepen one's passion and yearning for it.

Worshipers of popularity run to party after party, smiling politely, telling the same joke over and over, all the while carefully constructing a friendly, likable mask. But behind their performances are the painful questions of insecure children. "Do you like me? Am I OK? Do you find me acceptable?" Merton himself struggled with this over-sensitivity to the opinions of others, referring to it as his "allergy."[101]

In a Sunday afternoon lecture to his monastic community, Merton referred to this false god of popular approval as an "American trait" and a "special problem" which often dominates a person's life unconsciously. When it creeps into one's spiritual life, he noted the attention it commands and its divisive effects:

> It gets in the way of your freedom...and spiritual perception.... It will block you off. You will bring your energies over to this problem of pleasing somebody instead

[101] *Merton: By Those Who Knew Him Best*, ed. Paul Wilkes (San Francisco: Harper and Row, 1984), p. 96.

of going on with the thing that's really important. You can be easily diverted from the deep work.[102]

People who make the esteem of others a priority in life are hindered in discovering the true self. They are incapable of freely discerning and responding to their unique contribution to the Dream of the Kingdom. They need the permission of others. Though they usually appear as happy, fun-loving people, they are actually weak, shallow people who acquiesce and capitulate to the whims and dictates of others. Their opinions and actions change like the weather. These people are not their own persons. They are literally following someone else's agenda.

Society, upbringing or friends have taught us that self-esteem comes from a trim body, the doctoral diploma, the approval of others. Happiness is having the big house, the perfect spouse, the all-American children. Love means sex or sex means love. Domination and control display self-assurance. We have been deceived into thinking that we desperately need these twentieth-century golden calves in order to be happy. That is an illusion. That is the lie of the false self. That is the great temptation. Many of us spend the first half of our lives running after and worshipping these false gods. But God has cleverly programmed our emotional growth with the *grace* of the mid-life crisis.

At the crucial period of mid-life, the realization that the "eight P's" are not the "trump cards to success and happiness" comes crashing into our lives. We realize that they cannot make us happy. They are incapable of giving our lives meaning. They are false gods.

It was no doubt after his own mid-life crisis that Saint Paul wrote to the Philippians:

102 Merton, "Spiritual Direction."

Yet whatever gains I had, these I have come to regard as a loss because of Christ. More than that, I regard everything as loss because of the surpassing value of knowing Christ Jesus my Lord. For his sake I have suffered the loss of all things, and I regard them as rubbish, in order that I may gain Christ and be found in him.... (3:7-9a)

To proclaim God as Father in prayer is to proclaim God as Father by the way we live our lives. Practically speaking, that means refusing to get caught in the pigpen, the trap of the "eight P's," and returning home to an awareness of the true self, "Christ and being found in Christ," the Divine presence in which we dwell and that dwells within us.

Slavery and Addiction

We search for gods outside ourselves. To quote Merton's phrase, that keeps us "on the sidewalk outside the house." It compels us to dart and flit from one toy to another like bored little children. It drives us into the "bondage to decay" (Romans 8:21). And on a deeper level, it is a foolish denial of death.

Many of us unconsciously believe that we can become rich enough, powerful enough and famous enough to rob death of its sting. Granted we may not be so bold or naive as to verbalize this; yet our sins of idolatry proclaim it. At times we have to learn the hard way that "you can't take it with you when you die."

By a profound paradox, Sister Death teaches us the great existential truth that some people never learn in life: We are beggars. Indeed, the uneducated who attempt to pass over the threshold of this life to the next with lots of baggage and souvenirs, end up looking like fools. Take, for example, a millionaire in Boca Raton, Florida, whose final request, written in his will, was to be buried in his gold-plated

Cadillac, sitting in the driver's seat with a two-dollar cigar in his mouth and the air-conditioning turned on. His final wish was carried out to the last detail. "Now that's really living!" commented one gravedigger who witnessed this bizarre spectacle.

When we really believe that happiness is having it all, then we are no better than the millionaire trying to get into heaven with his gold-plated Cadillac. "[O]ne's life does not consist in the abundance of possessions" (Luke 12:15).

And every time we are envious or jealous of what other people have, we are no better than that gravedigger looking down with jealous admiration on that human corpse in an automobile.

Our worship of the "eight P's" is a humiliation for us. We obey the cares and desires of the ego and the flesh. We are in bondage to power and popularity. We are slaves to social approval and the prestige and status that come from piling up possessions. "For I do not do what I want, but I do the very thing I hate" (Romans 7:15b).

In effect, our hearts are not free. They are weighed down by the graven images which we think will make us happy. We think we need these idols so we trudge through life, pushing our possessions in abandoned grocery carts.

Part of the spiritual journey is breaking free from the conscious and unconscious hold that our attachments and passions, especially those addicted to the "eight P's," have upon us. It demands breaking the compulsion and emotional necessity to follow the agenda of the false self. This process traditionally has been called "mortification of the appetites" or "detachment."

The ancient Chinese philosopher Chuang Tzu speaks for all the great spiritual traditions when he describes the goal of mortification and detachment:

No drives, no compulsions,
No needs, no attractions:
Then your affairs
Are under control.
You are a free man.[103]

This is the "freedom of the glory of the children of God" (Romans 8:21). This is our vocation: "For freedom Christ has set us free.... [Y]ou were called to freedom" (Galatians 5:1, 13). This is the home of those rooted in the true self: "[W]here the Spirit of the Lord is, there is freedom" (2 Corinthians 3:17b). But its attainment comes with a price: radical heart surgery.

The Spiritual Cardiogram

Jesus says, "For where your treasure is, there your heart will be also" (Matthew 6:21). The spiritual cardiogram, based upon the insights of Anthony de Mello, S.J., can determine the depth of a person's obsession with and addiction to the "eight P's."

Here's how the "cardiogram" works: Spend some time alone. Journey into your heart. Think of your greatest treasure or prized possession. Maybe it's your house, automobile, spouse, children, friend, reputation, emotional health, status in life, job, or even image of God.

Once you have identified your "treasure," open the treasure chest of memories associated with it. Call to mind the many times you invested time, energy and money in enjoying it, promoting it and protecting it. Recall the good times and the difficult times connected with your treasure. Think of what it has done for you. Ponder the satisfaction

---

[103] Thomas Merton, *The Way of Chuang Tzu* (New York: New Directions, 1969), p. 112.

and pleasure it continues to give you.

Now, honestly and sincerely monitor your emotional, gut reactions to the following statements of wisdom:

- Your greatest treasure is your heaviest chain of slavery. Drop it and you're free!

- When you have lost your most prized possession, you have only lost a toy, a mere baby's rattle.

- Life is a banquet. The reason why there are so many hungry people in the world is because they prefer their toys over their meal.

The depth of your resistance to these truths reveals the degree to which you are in bondage to the "eight P's"—and in need of radical heart surgery. "[T]he gate is narrow and the road is hard that leads to life, and there are few who find it" (Matthew 7:14).

The Cure

I had been in the Franciscan Order for only four years. I can still remember the night during my theology studies when I heard a laywoman talk about her life of radical poverty. She was living on a very limited income, had only two dresses in her entire wardrobe and spent her life working with the poor on the streets of Chicago. I went back to the friary that night feeling guilty and depressed. Here I was, a Franciscan friar, someone who had freely vowed poverty as part of his daily life, who could spend ten or fifteen minutes in the morning trying to decide which of his many sweaters to wear that day. Guilt motivated me to look again at my understanding of poverty. I decided to give away a lot of my clothes and told my fellow friars I was opting for a simpler life-style.

The scavengers immediately showed up at my door and started taking shirts, sweaters and even my socks! The following day I woke up and started settling in to my poorer life-style. And it worked for awhile. I was happy with fewer things. I didn't worry as much. I was really quite peaceful. I kept telling myself, "Now I'm living like Saint Francis!" And in all humility, I took pride in that.

After about three weeks of "living like a saint," however, I became frustrated and angry. I resented watching others wear my shirts and sweaters. My blood would boil every time Tom said, "Albert, I really like these pants you gave me." I quickly came to regret my decision. And before long, there I was—buying new shirts, getting my hands on some new sweaters!

Simple renunciation does not break the deep, psychological chains of slavery to the "eight P's." Forbidden fruit always looks sweeter than the other selections on the menu. Like children, the more we are told we cannot have a certain item, the more we are curious about it, the more we think about it, the more we fantasize about it, and, in the end, the more we desire it.

Sheer willpower does not take away the deeper *craving*, *desire* and *taste* for it. Merton considered this trinity to be the source and root of our dissatisfaction in life.[104] To obliterate the deeper chain of desire, we must become emotionally indifferent to the "P." And indifference begins with the awareness that *things are not what they seem to be.*

Jesus' Beatitudes (Matthew 5:3-12) point explicitly to the fact that things are not what they seem to be. External "stuff" cannot bring happiness. Possessions and pride do not obtain what people think they do: "Blessed are the poor in spirit, for

---

[104] Thomas Merton, "The Spirit Gives Us Life," *The Merton Tapes* (Chappaqua, N.Y.: Electronic Paperbacks, 1972), tape 5, "Life and the Holy Spirit."

theirs is the Kingdom of heaven." Satisfied pleasures and emotional thrills cry out to be appeased again and again: "Blessed are those who mourn, for they will be comforted." Power is not what it seems to be: "Blessed are the meek, for they will inherit the earth"; "Blessed are the peacemakers, for they will be called children of God."

Matthew's Gospel, beginning with the Beatitudes, provides a commentary on the liberating insight and in so doing, offers a universal blueprint for holiness for Christians. Chapters five through seven directly confront the lies and illusions of the false self's agenda: mere external observance of the Law (5:21-48), false piety (6:1-4), spiritual workaholism (6:5-13), picking the scabs of hurts and grudges (6:14-15), false asceticism (6:16-18), a self-sufficient spirit that does not trust in the providence of God (6:19-21, 25-34), being inhospitable and demanding more from others than God has demanded from oneself (7:1-5), and the refusal to offer one's unique contribution to the Dream of the Kingdom (7:21-27). These three chapters unmask the thinking process of the false self and reveal its inner workings. They continually point to the great liberating insight which leads to the freedom of indifference.

The "eight P's" of the false self are not the elixirs of life. They do not give us what we think they will. They are lies and illusions. They are dangerous toys that sell us into slavery and compel our passions and desires. Our emotional attachment to them drives us right smack into the black hole of the false self. Freedom and the journey home begin with the realization and awareness that things are not what they seem to be.

The traditional three vows of religious life offer another commentary upon the Beatitudes. Though vowed explicitly by religious, they point to the freedom of indifference that is the challenge of all Christians. The vows are a radical renunciation and a resounding "no" to the agenda of the false self which equates happiness with the "eight P's." Poverty reveals the lie that possessions, productivity and comfort are the only means to happiness and inner peace. Humble obedience is a direct affront to the seductive deception that power, prestige, popularity and position are the measures of a person's worth in this world. Chastity is a sometimes painful reminder that there is no human being who can cure the restlessness of the human heart and make someone "happy ever after."

But these vows are more than a radical "no." Over time, as the vision of the vowed religious matures, these vows also become a resounding "yes" to the true self. Poverty declares the communal ownership of the goods of the earth. Chastity proclaims the communal identity of all creatures. Obedience heralds the unique contribution that each person is called to make for the preservation of God's Dream. Like the Beatitudes for all Christians, the vows of mature religious are vivid proclamations that external "stuff" found outside cannot make anyone really and truly happy. They remind a person of the only journey that is worth making in life, the journey home.

Augustine of Hippo

Augustine of Hippo was caught in the trap of the "eight P's" for some thirty years. In his *Confessions*, he relates how almost half his life was spent in idle and immoral pursuits. For thirty-three years he raced after prestige and knowledge, indulged his sexual desires and even fathered an illegitimate child. He was a deeply frustrated man, desperately looking outside himself for some god who could make him happy.

One day while Augustine read Scripture, the grace of God came into his life, and Augustine became aware of his bondage to the "eight P's." The words from Saint Paul's Letter to the Romans introduced him to another reality, the true self:

> Besides this, you know what time it is, how it is now the moment for you to wake from sleep. For salvation is nearer to us now than when we became believers; the night is far gone, the day is near. Let us then lay aside the works of darkness and put on the armor of light; let us live honorably as in the day, not in reveling and drunkenness, not in debauchery and licentiousness, not in quarreling and jealousy. Instead, put on the Lord Jesus Christ, and make no provision for the flesh, to gratify its desires. (13:11-14)

Augustine saw the "eight P's" for what they really were: lies, poison and the chains of his slavery. The words he wrote years later in his autobiography, *Confessions*, have become a classic text in the history of Christian spirituality:

> Late have I loved you, O Beauty, so ancient and so new, late have I loved you! And behold, you were within me and I was outside, and there I sought for you, and in my deformity I rushed headlong into the well-formed things that you have made. You were with me, and I was not with you. Those outer beauties held me far from you, yet if they had not been in you, they would not have existed at all. You called, and cried out to me and broke open my deafness; you shone forth upon me and you scattered my blindness: You breathed fragrance, and I drew in my breath and I now pant for you: I tasted and I hunger and thirst; you touched me, and I burned for Your peace.

Augustine, like Merton's madman, slept on the sidewalk outside his house instead of going inside where it is quiet and warm. Augustine spent years looking outside for the false gods that ultimately would never bring happiness to his heart. But the moment he began the interior journey,

Augustine made the great discovery. "You were within me and I was outside." That first step towards the true self began a life which Augustine described in this way: "You have made us for Yourself, O Lord, and our hearts are restless until they rest in You."

I saw a popular application of this great Augustinian insight on a billboard at the Dan Ryan Expressway and 55th Street in Chicago. Every week it contained a brief summary of the Gospel of the preceding Sunday. One weekday during Lent, I looked up to read the message. The Gospel that week was the Woman at the Well (John 4:4-42). In big black letters the billboard announced to all Chicago, "If you're thirsty, bring your bucket to Jesus!"

Brother Leo's 'P'

One day Saint Francis' longtime friend and companion, Brother Leo, was experiencing a serious temptation "not of the flesh but of the spirit." Perhaps he was feeling neglected, unloved, or not special in the eyes of Francis. Secretly, Brother Leo wished to have a special gift from the saint as a sign of favor and friendship and as a way to overcome this temptation of the spirit. He wanted a parchment, another "P." He no doubt thought that such a gift would make him happy. But like many a person both then and now, Brother Leo was embarrassed to ask his friend for such a gift.

Celano writes that the Holy Spirit revealed to Saint Francis the desire of Leo's heart. And so Francis wrote for Leo the "Praises of God," a prayer which is a reminder that nothing outside will satisfy the restlessness of the human heart—not even a friend's gift of a parchment![105] Revealing

---

[105] The story can be found in Celano's *Second Life* 49, *Omnibus of Sources*, p. 406.

to Brother Leo the secret of "not being led into the temptation" of idolatry, Francis prayed:

You are holy, Lord, the only God, You do wonders.
You are strong, You are great, You are the most high,
You are the almighty King.
You, Holy Father, the King of heaven and earth.
You are Three and One, Lord God of gods;
You are good, all good, the highest good,
Lord, God, living and true.
You are love, charity.
You are wisdom; You are humility; You are patience;
You are beauty; You are meekness; You are security;
You are inner peace; You are joy; You are our hope and joy.
You are justice; You are moderation; You are all our riches.
You are enough for us.
You are beauty, You are meekness;
You are the protector,
You are our guardian and defender;
You are strength; You are refreshment.
You are our hope, You are our faith, You are our charity.
You are all our sweetness,
You are our eternal life:
Great and wonderful Lord,
God almighty, Merciful Savior.

Points for Reflection

What is the most frequent sin in my life? How do I rationalize and justify it?

Which "P" is my addiction and source of slavery? What need or desire does this "P" fulfill in me? How can I best unmask its lie?

Take the spiritual cardiogram. What is my gut reaction to the three statements of wisdom?

How do I confront the false self's agenda by my living of the Beatitudes?

CHAPTER ELEVEN

'Do Not Subject Us to the Final Test But Deliver Us From the Evil One'

Matthew's version of the Lord's Prayer concludes with this last petition: "Do not subject us to the final test, but deliver us from the evil one" (6:13). According to Jewish apocalyptic thought, the endtime would be the time of Satan's final assault (see Revelation 3:10). There would be a final confrontation between believers and the power of evil. This "final test" would be so challenging, devastating and destructive that many people would fall away, give up the faith and lose all hope. Believing that God had lost interest and abandoned them, they would despair.

Jesus proclaimed the beginning of God's Kingdom where Satan no longer has any power or dominion. "But if it is by the finger of God that I cast out the demons, then the kingdom of God has come to you" (Luke 11:20). And to his followers, Jesus bequeathed this power and authority to defeat the prince of evil: "I watched Satan fall from heaven like a flash of lightning. See, I have given you authority to tread on snakes and scorpions, and over all the power of the enemy; and nothing will hurt you" (Luke 10:18).

A new springtime of invincible faith, hope and love had arrived when the Kingdom began with Jesus. There would now never be reason to give in to evil's illusion that Abba is disinterested or unapproachable. There would never be a situation that would warrant giving into the evil one's temptation towards hopelessness and despair. As Jesus had reminded his disciples at their last meal together, "In the world you face persecution. But take courage; I have conquered the world!" (John 16:33).

When an experience of life turns up the fire and tests our capacity to cope, whenever some situation pulls the carpet from underneath our feet, or when our whole world comes caving in, our great temptation is to forget the power that Jesus has given us and to despair. In Matthew's concluding petition to the Lord's Prayer, "O Lord, do not subject us to the final test," we are claiming the invincible hope that is ours even in the face of life's testings and trials. We are praying for patient endurance to overcome any temptation towards hopelessness and despair that the evil one places before us.

Scripture is filled with stories of people who are put to the test. The early Hebrews wandered in the desert for forty years and frequently complained to Moses that God had abandoned them (Exodus 14:11-12). Abraham experienced the agony of believing that God was calling him to sacrifice his own son, Isaac (Genesis 22:1-19). In the Garden of Gethsemane, Jesus was filled with doubts and fears and even asked his Abba to spare him from drinking the cup of suffering (Luke 22:39-46). And with barely any physical strength left within his body, the crucified Jesus cried aloud the words of the Psalmist, "My God, my God, why have you forsaken me?" (Mark 15:33-37).

Like the Hebrews, we too have wandered endlessly in the desert. We have also had our moments of confusion when we did not know which road to follow on our life's journey. We have all had the experience of walking endlessly and yet getting nowhere. Like Abraham, we have felt called to let go of someone or something very dear and precious to us: a job in which we invested so much of our time and energy; a loved one in death; friends and familiar surroundings when we move to another city. Like Jesus, most of us have experienced at least one tragedy in life when we momentarily lost our faith in God and wondered, "Where are you, God? Have you forgotten me?"

So what do we do when we experience "the test" or "evil's trial" in our life? Surrender and trust: These are the only two responses that rob any trial of its power to destroy us.

All four Gospels agree that once Judas and the crowd arrived in the Garden of Gethsemane, Jesus did nothing to defend himself. He simply followed the very advice that the evangelists remembered him giving his disciples. He picked up his cross.

With shocking deliberateness, Jesus bowed before the mystery of suffering and gave himself over into the hands of his executioners. He surrendered and embraced the cross. And in that gracious surrender to the way of the cross, in that deliberate acceptance of the *via dolorosa*, Jesus showed us how to turn pain into praise and suffering into the song of salvation.

True and Perfect Joy

Francis of Assisi once made the same point to Brother Leo. Francis began by telling his friend and confessor explicitly what true joy does *not* consist in: the brotherhood attracting scholars, bishops and kings; the friars converting all the nonbelievers to the Christian faith; the presence of a certain friar with the special grace to heal the sick or perform miracles. When Brother Leo, somewhat puzzled, asked,

"What then is perfect joy?" Francis replied:

> I return from Perugia and arrive here in the dead of night; and it is winter time, muddy and so cold that icicles have formed on the edges of my habit and keep striking my legs, and blood flows from such wounds. And all covered with mud and cold, I come to the gate and after I have knocked and called for some time, a brother comes and asks: "Who are you?" I answer: "Brother Francis." And he says: "Go away; this is not a proper hour for going about; you may not come in." And when I insist, he answers: "Go away, you are a simple and a stupid person; we are so many and we have no need of you. You are certainly not coming to us at this hour!" And I stand again at the door and say: "For the love of God, take me in tonight." And he answers: "I will not. Go to the Crosiers' place and ask there." I tell you this: If I had patience and did not become upset, there would be true joy in this and true virtue and the salvation of the soul.[106]

What a startling reversal of values! Francis says true and perfect joy is found in our response to the cross of rejection, the cross of betrayal, the cross of inconvenience.

The false self is easily threatened and considers its reputation at stake in every situation. Rather than surrender to the cross and trust in the grace of God, the false self has the emotional need to take a stand and fight. It immediately draws the battle lines. It would view the brother who answers the door as the enemy to be defeated. Anger, revenge and intolerance are its weapons as it seeks to defend itself and make its presence known. It is motivated by self-justification and vindication.

The false self *reacts* to another person; it does not respond. As Merton says, the self-assertion of the false self is egocentric: "It starts and ends with *me*, my desire." In contrast, "My real self is the last thing in the world that I

---

[106] *Francis and Clare*, pp. 165-166.

have to affirm.... It's not something that *I* have to make or give or create. It's *given*."[107]

Matthew's concluding petition, "Do not subject us to the final test but deliver us from the evil one" is a prayer to renounce the kind of self-assertion, violent reaction and self-vindication that characterizes the agenda of the false self. It is a prayer to find my way back home, to the true self.

The true self does not have an emotional need to make a personal statement, take a stand, justify and defend itself. As Merton told the monks of Gethsemani, "The more you develop [in the spiritual life], the less you have to prove."[108] The true self simply submits and surrenders. As Christ did on the cross, the true self stops the cycle of violent self-assertion and absorbs the other's evil within itself.

Mary's son had been brutally murdered in cold blood in Boston. When asked if she wanted to pursue the death penalty in court, Mary replied, "No. Let the violence stop with the murder of my son." To quote the words of Jesus, "Do not resist an evildoer. But if anyone strikes you on the right cheek, turn the other also" (Matthew 5:39).

Some forms of pain and suffering—like those we experience as a result of our need to control and manipulate the situations we find ourselves in—are the prices we pay to keep the false self alive and thriving. But other forms of suffering confront the false self head-on and unmask its illusions and lies. When we surrender to a "test" and trust in the fidelity of God, we are renouncing the agenda of the false self and coming a step closer to home, to the true self. We are choosing to accept, validate and live in the sacrament of the present moment. This, according to the Franciscan tradition,

[107] Thomas Merton, "Prayer and the Active Life" (Kansas City, Mo.: Credence Cassettes), tape AA 2072.
[108] Merton, "Spiritual Direction."

is the meaning of true and perfect joy and the salvation of the soul.

In Admonition 13 Francis states that a person's patience and humility are not measured in times of grace but in times of trials. Francis says a person only knows how much patience and humility a friar has when "those who should do him justice, do quite the opposite to him."

In Admonition 14 Francis speaks about those people who spend long hours in prayer, do many acts of penance and mortification, and perform many good deeds yet, as soon as someone speaks a word against them or threatens to take something from them, they become angry and scandalized. The false self has a need to react and protect. Francis concludes by stating that these supposedly pious friars are not poor in spirit. "People who are truly poor in spirit hate themselves [Luke 14:26] and love those who strike them on the cheek [Matthew 5:39]." One's ultimate attachment to the values of the true self or the false self appears in times of trials.

In his gracious surrender to the way of the cross, in his deliberate acceptance of the *via dolorosa*, Jesus showed us how to turn pain into praise and some forms of suffering into the song of salvation. As Chardin says, "Surrender to suffering as though it were a loving energy." Surrender and trust: These are the only two responses that rob any cross of its power to destroy us.

Suffering as Song: The Canticle of Creatures

The last two years of Francis' life are very well documented in the memories of Brothers Leo, Angelo and Rufino, the small group of friars who cared for the saint in the last years of his life. According to the *Legend of Perugia*,

Francis spent more than fifty days at San Damiano in a small hut that was infested with mice. These mice tormented the now-blind and frail saint during his prayer and even got up onto the table and ate from his plate at meal times. The early companions tell us that Francis went into a depression and started feeling sorry for himself. He prayed for hope and patient endurance in the face of his cross. Francis heard these words in response from God, "Brother, be glad and joyful in the midst of your infirmities and tribulations. As of now, live in peace as if you were already sharing my kingdom."[109] Upon receiving these words of consolation from God, Francis cast aside his self-pity and stopped fighting against the sickness, his blindness and the mice. Like Jesus whom he constantly tried to imitate, Francis accepted the cross of the present moment and trusted that God would keep the Divine promise and not abandon a servant.

Swimming in that very "Kingdom moment," Francis renounced the false self's compulsion to control and change the situation. From that stance, he suddenly became aware of the Divine presence that surrounded him like the air he breathed. The blind saint saw creation in all its ordinariness and sacramentality. It became a ladder for him. The sun was the bringer of the light of day—and also a reflection of God!

> Praised be You, my Lord, with all your creatures, especially Sir Brother Sun, Who is the day and through whom You give us light. He is beautiful and radiant with great splendor; he bears a likeness of You, Most High One.

The saint recognized the family of creation: Sister Moon, Brother Wind, Sister Water, Brother Fire, Sister Mother Earth. He again experienced God as Almsgiver and himself as

---

[109] *Legend of Perugia* 43, *Omnibus of Sources*, p. 1020.

beggar: "Through every kind of weather, You give sustenance to Your creatures." He gave praise to Sister Death whom he no longer feared; he referred to her as "the second death," the first, no doubt, being the moment when he began enouncing the "eight P's" of the false self before the bishop and citizens of Assisi. And, in this tremendous moment of enlightenment, Francis became more deeply rooted in the true self as he rediscovered who he already was and who he was called to be: a humble servant of God's will. "Praise and bless my Lord and give Him thanks and serve Him with great humility."

The Canticle of Creatures is Francis' resurrection song in the face of his own Good Friday. In the saint's gracious surrender to the cross and his act of fervent trust in God, agony became adoration, pain became praise, and suffering quite literally became song.

'Take Up Your Cross'

"Whoever wishes to come after me must deny the self, take up the cross, and follow me." That is the one requirement Jesus places upon anyone who wishes to be his disciple. It is direct and unequivocal, and the Gospel tradition repeats it five times (Mark 8:34, Matthew 10:38, 16:24, Luke 9:23, 14:27).

Jesus does not simply encourage us to have hope and not to despair before the cross. He commands us to actively embrace it!

What is it about surrendering and accepting the crosses of our testings and trials that makes them so important— even the prerequisite for Christian discipleship?

Brother Thomas of Celano states that, early on, the cross was imprinted upon the heart of Francis, and each day and night the saint would spend time meditating and pondering it.[110] Francis fell so deeply in love with the cross, Celano writes, that his heart could no longer contain its affection. It burst open and the cross, planted as a seed in the saint's body, sprouted and bore fruit in the external wounds of the stigmata.[111]

Bonaventure divides Francis' life into seven segments, each containing an apparition of the cross. For Bonaventure, the cross is the summary of Francis's entire life. He says of Francis:

> You can make your boast in the glory of the Cross without fear now, O glorious standard-bearer of the Cross! It was from the Cross you began, and according to the rule of the Cross that you made progress, and it was in the Cross that you brought your life to its final consummation.[112]

Why is it so essential to surrender to the cross, "to carry it about continuously" in one's heart, as Bonaventure puts it elsewhere?[113] These questions hounded me for years. But the Zen masters have a saying, "When the disciple is ready, the master appears." My master was Margo.

It was a cold Wednesday afternoon in January, 1986, two weeks before Margo died. She lay in the hospital bed that her parents had bought and placed in the family's living room. She was only sixteen years old and she was dying of Lou Gehrig's disease. What immediately struck me was the clarity of her eyes and the simplicity of her smile. A silent beauty radiated from her diseased body.

I felt very awkward and had no idea what to say. But, with a cordial sensitivity that set me at ease immediately, she

---

[110] Ibid., *Second Life* 10-11, pp. 370-371.
[111] Ibid., 211, p. 530.
[112] Ibid., *Miracles* 10:9, p. 787.
[113] *Tree of Life* Prol. 1.

faced the issue squarely and bluntly—the very issue about which I had been asked to talk with her yet did not know how to broach. With a soft voice in which I could not detect any self-pity, she asked, "I guess they told you I am dying, huh?"

I nodded my head. "Yes."

She calmly stated that the time must be getting close because she noticed her breathing was becoming more and more difficult. She explained that this muscular disease would cause her to gradually lose control of her lungs and, in the end, she would suffocate.

I was taken aback by her bluntness. I searched my mind and heart for something to say, and these are the words, I am now embarrassed to admit, that tumbled out of my mouth. "Margo, do you find it hard to die?"

"Not really," she replied instantly. "The suffering of the past year has forced me to let go of so many trivial concerns. It has taught me simply to trust in God because, really, that's all I have left—my faith in God's goodness and mercy. I don't even pray for a miracle to be cured because somehow or another, I trust—or maybe I know—that this disease is supposed to be my way to heaven.

"Since my suffering has taught me to depend so completely upon God here on earth," Margo said, "I suspect death will simply be a continuation of the way I've been living for the past year. And so, no, Father, I'm really not afraid to die. And I don't think it will be hard. I suspect it will come quite naturally to me."

Margo gave me the answer to my question. Jesus told us to embrace the cross because that is how we learn to open our hearts in hospitality and trust to God and others. The cross is painful and causes frustration in our lives because it challenges and attacks the very values that are prized by the false self: independence, heartless reasoning, control of life and manipulation of others. It both forces us and teaches us to let go, surrender and trust. And when we do that, we can even face the finality of death as Margo did and say, "Where, O death, is your victory? Where, O death, is your sting?" (1 Corinthians 15:55). The very moment we surrender, pain becomes praise. Weakness becomes strength.

Then Margo seemingly contradicted all she had just said by adding, "Yes. It's hard to die." She spoke of how deeply hurt her parents and friends would be by her death. She spent much of our time together that afternoon telling me how her death was going to be a tragedy and trial for her loved ones. "How will my parents cope? How will my friends be able to get on with their lives after I'm gone?" I could not help but see the irony in the whole situation: In the face of her own suffering and death, Margo was worried and concerned about how others would deal with the loss of her presence.

Maybe that is why Jesus insisted that we pick up our crosses every day if we want to be his followers. The crosses of life can teach us compassion and how to be sensitive to the sufferings of others. They make us vividly aware of the fact that everyone is wounded and crucified in some way. Our crosses are the seeds of our compassion. They can transform hearts of stone into bread, able to be broken for the hungry of the world.

When Margo took the focus away from her own physical pain and responded to the grief that others were going to experience at her death, the bitter cross of Lou Gehrig's disease suddenly lost its power to destroy and was converted into an instrument of loving compassion and a channel of salvation. Indeed, what was written of the Suffering Servant could also be written of Margo:

Surely [she] has borne our infirmities
   and carried our diseases;
yet we accounted [her] stricken,
   struck down by God, and afflicted.
...[B]y [her] bruises we are healed. (Isaiah 53:4, 5)

When we surrender to the cross with faith, when we allow its pain and sorrow to move us beyond self-pity to sensitivity for the sufferings of others, we become like Francis of Assisi, Margo and so many others in this world. We develop a profound respect for all creation and a profound love and compassion for other people. We are able to grasp an insight and an appreciation for the curious words of Saint Paul:

> May I never boast of anything except the cross of our Lord Jesus Christ, by which the world has been crucified to me, and I to the world. ...[L]et no one make trouble for me; for I carry the marks of Jesus branded on my body. (Galatians 6:14, 17)

As I left Margo's home that January afternoon, a concluding sentence from an article I had read years before suddenly popped into my mind: "Talk to the dying; they will teach you how to live." I paused before turning the ignition of the car and prayed, knowingly, the prayer of Saint Peter Damien:

> Lord, set the seal of your holy cross upon my soul and cleanse me by its power. By its merits, claim me wholly and entirely for yourself. When you come to judge the world, may its imprint be found upon me. Thus, likened to my Crucified Lord in his sufferings, I may be found worthy to share his glorious resurrection.

Hope

Surrender and acceptance are only part of the required response to rob any cross of its power to destroy us. We must also fan the flame of hope. We must trust in God. Why? Our personal experiences of the desert, of Gethsemane and of Calvary are never simply times of testing. As our Judeo-Christian tradition has shown time and time again, times of trial are also times when God once again proclaims that he has not forgotten or abandoned us, that he really is an Abba who is invested in the life of each one of us. As Thomas Merton writes:

> For perfect hope is achieved on the brink of despair when, instead of falling over the edge, we find ourselves walking on the air. Hope is always just about to turn into despair, but never does so, for at the moment of supreme crisis God's power is suddenly made perfect in our infirmity.[114]

When I find myself falling over the edge in times of testing or tragedy, I pray, "Do not subject us to the final test, but deliver us from the evil one." And the promise of God will provide wings for me, the beloved. "Can a woman forget her nursing child, or show no compassion for the child of her womb? Even these may forget, yet I will not forget you" (Isaiah 49:15).

God's covenant with us is eternal and unconditional. God will always be present to us as savior and deliverer. Abba is on our side. Abba will never forget, abandon or forsake us. That is the deepest meaning of grace. When everything falls apart and our world comes caving in, God enters and manifests the Divine presence. Indeed, the hand of God transforms testings, trials and tragedies into moments

---

[114] Merton, *No Man Is an Island*, p. 157.

of amazing grace. That is the story of Easter resurrection. Despite what Jesus screamed from the cross, Abba did not abandon his beloved Son. Abba was quietly there, waiting for the right moment. "Do not be afraid; I know that you are looking for Jesus who was crucified. He is not here; for he has been raised, as he said" (Matthew 28:5-6).

After a few spiritual direction sessions with Linda, I knew something was brewing inside of her. And many clues were beginning to suggest a most horrible reality: sexual abuse. Though I did not want to make her feel further isolated and abandoned, I was also aware that the issue was well beyond my own competence. I suggested she pursue counseling, and she soon entered a six-month inpatient holistic health program.

In a short Christmas letter, Linda wrote that she was facing many areas of her life which were both frightening and painful. "Between the group sessions, the individual counseling sessions and my spiritual direction appointments, I find myself broken into many pieces that are scattered in different meeting rooms down the hallway. It's hard work. Pray for me."

Around mid-April, I received a lengthy letter written the Monday during Holy Week. She only had ten days left in the program and was looking forward to getting back into the rhythm of life. She felt good, vibrant. "I've rediscovered myself." She concluded that letter with words which still bring a smile to my face: "P.S. God surely didn't let me down. Celebrate with me. I feel Easter in my bones."

Andrew's ten years of denying his alcoholism had destroyed his first marriage, wrecked two automobiles, and was on the verge of destroying his second marriage. I called him on the phone the first night after he was released from a sixty-day program for addiction in a local hospital. When I asked him about his newfound sobriety, all he could quote were the words of Jackie Gleason on the *Honeymooners*: "How sweet it is!" Then Andrew added, "God is good and getting better every day."

Jean Marie was a very active woman and a nurse by profession. At the age of thirty-five, she was diagnosed on the operating table with a rare disease that causes degeneration of a person's spinal cord. The doctors could not tell her how long she could continue living her active life-style before crutches, braces and orthopedic shoes would be her lot.

Jean Marie went into a deep depression. She feared how she would ultimately end up. Since there is currently no cure for the disease, she knew it was just a matter of time until she ended up in a wheelchair or lay bedridden.

That was seventeen years ago. When I met Jean Marie for the first time, she was wearing orthopedic shoes and a stiff neck brace. She had been told to spend at least half her waking hours sitting in a chair. But amazingly, Jean Marie is totally at peace with her disease and the inconvenience that is now part of her daily routine. She told me that it took nearly one full year to get out of the initial depression and to reconcile herself to the inevitable: The disease was not going to disappear; she would have to accept it. Over a period of twelve months, her pain became praise and her suffering became song as she surrendered to the disease and trusted that God would stay near to her. In the words of her own Magnificat, "Where the grace of God has brought me, the grace of God will keep me."

Each of these stories illustrates the saving power of God in the midst of a trial, test or human infirmity. Grace brings forth life from suffering and death. Grace gives us the courage to accept what we cannot change. Grace makes the impossible suddenly possible. It appears as a miraculous solution in the throes of a devastating problem. It causes something to "shift" internally and life becomes worth living again. It is the foundation of our trust.

Trust in God's power and grace can never be overdone since no situation is too complex, too complicated, or too convoluted for God. It is never too late for a miracle because Divine power can write straight with crooked lines. Grace is always waiting around the corner for the right moment. Thus, Saint Paul could write unabashedly to the Corinthians:

> We are afflicted in every way, but not crushed; perplexed, but not driven to despair; persecuted, but not forsaken; struck down, but not destroyed; always carrying in the body the death of Jesus, so that the life of Jesus may also be made visible in our bodies. (2 Corinthians 4:8-10)

To proclaim God as Abba in prayer is to proclaim God as the Abba of amazing grace. As absurd, irresponsible and naive as it may sound, those rooted in the true self will surrender and trust in the face of every Gethsemane and Good Friday. When they pray, "Do not subject us to the final test, but deliver us from the evil one," they are filled with unshakable patience and invincible hope. No matter where they are, no matter what situation they find themselves in, they know who they really are: These are the beloved. They have captured Divine attention. There's nothing more they need. So they remain as lovers in Abba's house, in the sacrament of the present moment.

Points for Reflection

What have been the key moments of testing in my life? How did I respond to them? Was I able to overcome the temptation to lose hope?

Do I promote the false self's agenda by constantly taking a stand, justifying and defending myself? Do I have an emotional need to be vindicated?

When has pain become praise in my life?

Do I have a devotion to the cross? How do I "take up the cross" to follow Jesus?

Do I believe in grace? In miracles? Do I remain a person of invincible hope?

Conclusion

This book has used the words of the Lord's Prayer as a springboard for a new approach to spirituality. This spirituality can be well described by Thomas Merton's words for his own experiences of praying the Our Father: It is like "swimming in the heart of the sun." Swimming is a dynamic and yet very ordinary experience. It involves concentration, awareness and enjoyment. It implies an involvement and cooperation between human effort and the sheer grace of movement. "In the heart of the sun" means that Merton's kind of swimming occurs at the very center, one could say at "ground zero," of the physical life-source.

"Swimming in the heart of the sun" is an apt image for the five components of spirituality:

Image of God. Perhaps the most important aspect of my spiritual life is my personal image of God. God lives "in heaven" and his name is so "hallowed" that no one image or word can ever adequately describe the Divine reality. That's why my image of God should change as I grow and mature and come to experience God in a variety of ways. Jesus drew from one of a child's most intimate, dynamic and ordinary relationships to portray his experience of God. He called God "*Abba.*"

The Abba of Jesus is a God of love. That love is all-encompassing, unconditional and surrounds me like the rays of the sun, like the air I breathe. I am the beloved! That is the reality of life and that is all I really need; that awareness is the goal of prayer.

The Abba of Jesus is also a God of mercy and compassion. He "forgives our trespasses" and forgets them with the bat of an eye. He holds no grudges. He refuses to live in the past. I am called to celebrate that same mercy and forgiveness—"to forgive those who trespass against us"—by the way I live my life and respond to those who hurt and betray me.

This loving God is the source of all the good things in my life—from my "daily bread" to my gifts, talents and actions. I am a beggar, totally dependent upon God. That awareness leads me to make Mary's words my own, "The Lord has done good things for me and holy is the name!"

Community. Jesus taught that his Abba is also *our* Abba. I am a member of Abba's beloved family.

As a child in Abba's family of humanity, I am called to stretch the size of my heart so that it mirrors more and more God's loving heart. I too give life to others, especially the poor and needy, as I intercede for them through prayer and my acts of compassion. And I proclaim Abba as my own source of love and life through my hospitality for all, including the family of creation.

Commitment. Such a precious gift of life, love and mercy calls forth from me the challenge to preserve God's Dream of peace, justice and love by witnessing and praying, "Thy Kingdom come!" One of the most important ways that I do that is by doing "God's will on earth as it is in heaven"; the major decisions of my life are discerned and oriented towards God's Kingdom.

That commitment becomes the driving force around my celebration of the Eucharist. The "daily bread" that Abba provides for me is the same bread that I am challenged to become for others—in small ways, in heroic ways. I am a eucharistic person called to be broken for the sake of God's Dream.

Asceticism. But that challenge and commitment do not come easily to me. Like the prodigal son, I have wandered far from my home in pursuit of my own will, my own desires, my own false gods. That is the result of sin in the world; that is the source of so much of my frustration and restlessness. And that has created the false self which Jesus says must die.

My commitment to God's Kingdom demands the price of asceticism—renouncing the false gods, especially the "eight P's," that weigh me down and constantly sell me into slavery. My prayer, "Lead us not into temptation," becomes an expression of my lifelong renunciation. And that renunciation provides glimmers of my true self, the free and upright child created in the image of God.

The present moment as an encounter with God. As I leave my pigpen and begin the journey back to my true self, I gradually grow in the awareness of the great insight of the spiritual life: There is nothing to get "somewhere else" because I already have it right here!

That insight is grounded in the Incarnation of Jesus Christ, the great reality of God made flesh. The unique marriage of Creator and creature, of grace and nature, reveals to me the sacramentality of all creation and the annunciation of every moment of my life. Angels come; angels go— incarnated in flesh and blood. And, all the while, I experience the grace and love of Abba that fills me, as Catherine of Siena said, "like the ocean fills the fish."

Because of this Divine attention which is always riveted upon me and my family, I am truly "delivered from the evil" of hopelessness and despair. In the midst of my tests and trials, there is only one authentic response: surrender to the present. And in that response of my true self, my pain becomes praise and my suffering becomes song.

For those who come back home to the sacrament of the present, filled with the light and unconditional love of God, every moment is an experience of "swimming in the heart of the sun"!